What people are saying about …

# NEW MAN JOURNEY

"At sixty years of age, I know that one of the most challenging and rewarding parts of life is keeping an eternal perspective while pursuing your dreams. Steve Silver understands the importance of keeping your focus on God and how that becomes the true measure of ultimate success."

**Rick Scott,** governor of Florida

"What is the meaning of life? Are we the men we want to be? *New Man Journey* takes a penetrating look at how we can be transformed from ordinary to extraordinary. Understanding ourselves is the first step in this process. Steve Silver deals with practical examples of who we really are on the inside. This allows each of us to begin the process of becoming the New Men we need to be."

**Murray D. Martin,** chairman, president, and CEO of Pitney Bowes

"In *New Man Journey*, Stevow to have a more fulfilling, purpment. In God's kingdom, our works the excitement and anticipationreach

others with the love of Christ. I highly recommend this book for those in or nearing retirement."

**Ralph Reed,** chairman of The Faith and Freedom
Coalition and author of *Ballots and Blood, The
Confirmation, Dark Horse,* and *Active Faith*

"One thing has certainly been true in my life: the moments when I learn *most* are the times when I'm *least* comfortable. Steve pushes you past your comfort zone, but what follows are deeper levels of learning, appreciation, and loving. I'm so glad that I decided to buckle up and take this ride."

**Mike Whan,** LPGA commissioner (and
late bloomer on faith's wonderful ride)

"When we get to the second half of our lives, all of us have a choice: to coast and drift or to dig deep for greater meaning and purpose. The former is easy. The latter requires more work. If that truth resonates, then *New Man Journey* is the book for you. It is authentic, readable, interesting, insightful, and really, really practical. Steve Silver goes to the heart of life's most important questions: Why are we here? What should we do next?"

**Brian Hall,** professor of
business administration at
Harvard Business School

"*New Man Journey* asks questions that most of us think about but don't often grapple with. To grow in Christ and become more effective in serving Him we need to be truly transformed. That's not always a comfortable process. I highly recommend this book for any man who is ready to raise the bar on his Christian commitment and walk."

**Wayne Huizenga Jr.,** president
of Huizenga Holdings, Inc.

*"New Man Journey* is a winner! Steve Silver presents us with an opportunity to exhibit authentic, honest, and transparent lives."

**Bob Doll,** former chief equity strategist
at Blackrock Investment Management

"If you are looking to find your fire in retirement, then you need to read this book."

**Steve Reinemund,** dean of Wake Forest
University School of Business and former
chairman and CEO of Pepsico

*"New Man Journey* is an excellent book for men of all ages, but especially those in their retirement years. Steve Silver knows men. God has given him a heart and a vision in this special phase of life, which has manifested itself in the Men's Golf Fellowship that he started in southwest Florida ten years ago. Steve knows God in his personal walk and in his ministry. All who read this book will know God better and grow in their relationships with Him. *New Man Journey* is vital for men who are seeking to know who they are and what they should do with the rest of their lives."

**Dr. Paul Dixon,** chancellor of
Cedarville University

"*New Man Journey* is for anyone who has matured enough to realize that no career, no material possession, and no relationship can fill the emptiness that ultimately every man and woman faces. Indeed, having faced it myself, I highly recommend this book because it tells the truth that only Jesus Christ can take away our emptiness and replace it with love, joy, and peace."

**Michael Timmis,** chairman of
Prison Fellowship International and
author of *Between Two Worlds*

"Steve Silver spent his career as a management consultant solving problems for others. In *New Man Journey,* he applies his deep understanding of the Christian faith and the Bible to help men live retirement lives of purpose and joy. It is absorbing reading, with stories and illustrations that bring home the message that 'you must be born again to experience fullness of life.' If things just aren't the way you expected in retirement, then I'd heartily recommend you read this book."

**Alistair Hanna,** founding chairman
of Alpha USA and former managing
director of McKinsey & Company

"I have been thrilled to watch Steve Silver's own 'New Man Journey' from material success to community and ministry significance. This engaging, lively, and very personal book will ignite men of all stages and ages to be high-impact players for eternity and to sprint the last lap of life's race. Even if you think you are 'old,' you can become new. Warning: the complacent are in for a blessed disturbance! To paraphrase a wise man, 'God loves you as you are, but doesn't want to leave you as you are.'"

**Dr. Hayes Wicker,** senior pastor of
First Baptist Church Naples

"Steve Silver's *New Man Journey* is a wonderful book! The Spirit of Christ is throughout its pages. This book is for people of all ages, but it is a must read for retired men. I couldn't put it down. Now I find myself going back and rereading sections that inspired me."

**Peter Thomas,** announcer and narrator
of television, radio, and film

"Steve Silver's insights are relevant not only to men who haven't yet opened up to Christ. What he shares, from his own life and from the composites of those he has interacted with, applies to all men wherever they may be in their life's journey. This book is a mirror for us to see ourselves; it helps us face the truth about who we are and points the way to change and growth. Like most men, I have recurring feelings that there has to be 'something more' to life than I've experienced. Steve helps me to see what that 'more' is, and how to find it."

**Dr. Doug Pratt,** senior pastor of First
Presbyterian, Bonita Springs

"Steve has written a book from his life's experiences that will impact men and women in or about to enter the second half of their lives. Steve's passion to help men and women experience and achieve more meaningful and fulfilling lives comes through every page. If you want a new perspective on how to enrich your relationships with your spouse, family, and friends, this book is for you."

**Michael Cardone Jr.,** founder and
chairman of Cardone Industries and
author of *Business with Soul*

*"New Man Journey* is compelling, provocative, emotionally unsettling, meaningful, and uplifting. It speaks softly yet powerfully to all of us who are continually striving for purpose and passion in this retirement phase of our life journeys. As Steve makes clear, this is a quest that is much easier said than done. As our new 'wardrobe' may now include Tommy Bahama shirts, iPads, and hybrid clubs, 'putting on Christ' (as Steve affirms) in our own individual way is the only certain path to meaningful reconciliation, relationship, and transformation!"

**Joe Frick,** vice chairman and managing partner
of Diversified Search, LLC and vice chairman
and former CEO of Independence Blue Cross

"Steve's persistent style and his passion to champion change is a model for all of us to follow. It is so easy to coast through the second phase of life. Steve shows us that we are not finished and how we can be examples and mentors ... It is so refreshing to read a book that challenges us to help others and make the next phase truly rewarding by adopting 'giving back' as our life motto. A truly inspirational read."

**Bob Lawless,** chairman and CEO of
Opportunity International, Canada, and former
chairman and CEO of McCormick & Company

"Steve Silver is amazingly direct and penetrating in his quest to be helpful to men. While this book is directed at those nearing or in retirement, it speaks powerfully to men and women of all ages. Steve captures your heart with relevant and real stories that resonate deep in your soul. This is not just another book for retirees but a life changer that should be required reading. Steve gets it! Don't miss out on hearing the practical truth that so many miss in life."

**Hal Rosser,** founding partner of
Rosser Capital Partners, LP

"I have yet to meet a man who hasn't struggled with the age-old battle between his lower and higher natures—or one who has found that transformation easy. *New Man Journey* provides us with a powerful yet practical guided tour through the 'dragon's cave' of our Old Man to ultimate victory in our New Man in Christ. This is an extraordinary book—amazing in its honesty and transparency. Get ready for the best journey you'll ever take."

**Tom Randall,** chaplain of Champion's Tour

"Sadly, many endure this entire life on earth eagerly awaiting the glories of heaven but not understanding all that God has for us now. This book is not about the power to get you to heaven—it is about the power to get heaven to you. No need to wait for the New Earth to be a New Man. God can do it now."

**Tim Philpot,** judge serving Fayette
Circuit Court, Lexington, and former
president of CBMC International

"Steve Silver's *New Man Journey* grapples with the way we can live out the later days of our lives in service to the Lord, our family, and our colleagues. This frank and compelling book will help Christians make sense of the competing worldviews that clamor for our attention in a pluralistic society. *New Man Journey* weaves together engaging stories with penetrating analysis of ideas that will help Christians defend their faith and live out its full implications in every area of life."

**Dallen Peterson,** founder of Merry Maids
and author of *Rags, Riches, and Real Success*

"Ephesians 4:22–24 tells us to put off the old man and put on the new man. Steve's book is a step-by-step guide for doing just that! *New Man Journey* is a timely book that captures the essence of that flesh-spirit struggle we all have and walks us through the journey using Scripture, story, and personal insight. Steve's conversational style engages, his incisive questions challenge, and the gripping analogies throughout help guide the reader down the path of understanding not only how we deceive ourselves, but also what it truly means to live a life that matters forever."

**J. Blake Brown,** pastor of Southwest
Harbor Congregational Church

"Steve Silver's *New Man Journey* is a powerful and extremely useful book for Christian men who seek greater fulfillment from their lives."

**Bob Tedeschi,** contributing columnist
to *The New York Times*

"If you are a man approaching or at retirement age and you want to finish well from an eternal perspective, *New Man Journey* is a must read. Steve Silver has authored an engaging, challenging, and convicting book through weaving stories into the tapestry of our self-perception in such an effective manner that it seems he is speaking to us personally. You will be motivated to move beyond previous successes (and failures) and to get in the real game of life today and tomorrow—pressing on toward the goal to win the prize for which God has called you heavenward."

**Don Patterson,** chairman of Good
News Jail & Prison Ministry and
founder and former CEO of 3Com

"Ever have the feeling that there should be more to life than this? Steve Silver's *New Man Journey* leads the way to lasting, satisfying change: from routine to revitalized living, from stagnant to reconciled relationships, from a self-centered Old Man to a Christ-centered New Man. This is a book for every guy—no matter his age—who wants to make the rest of his life the best of his life."

**James Lund,** editor, author, and coauthor
of *A Dangerous Faith* and *Danger Calling*

"*New Man Journey* should be required reading for anyone, man or woman, who is seeking the answer to the meaning of life. That is a strong statement, however, knowing God's Son is the answer to every question. As Steve so eloquently states, we can never really know Jesus until we remove the Old Man and replace him with the

New Man. Following the simple admonitions that Steve lays out would revolutionize our society."

**Randy Kington,** retired USMC and
CPA and author of *What a Life*

"I have known Steve since the onset of Men's Golf Fellowship and observed his passion to share Christ in this unique ministry, and I use *passion* in the strictest sense of the word. *New Man Journey* accurately depicts the process of moving from a successful career to a transformed life and dealing with that empty hole that can be filled only by Christ. This book is a blessing to read."

**Donald Mitchell,** retired executive of
General Motors Corporation and former
chairman of CBMC International

# NEW MAN JOURNEY

## FINDING MEANING IN RETIREMENT

# STEVE SILVER

David C Cook®
transforming lives together

NEW MAN JOURNEY
Published by David C Cook
4050 Lee Vance View
Colorado Springs, CO 80918 U.S.A.

David C Cook Distribution Canada
55 Woodslee Avenue, Paris, Ontario, Canada N3L 3E5

David C Cook U.K., Kingsway Communications
Eastbourne, East Sussex BN23 6NT, England

The graphic circle C logo is a registered trademark of David C Cook.

The website addresses recommended throughout this book are offered as a
resource to you. These websites are not intended in any way to be or imply an
endorsement on the part of David C Cook, nor do we vouch for their content.

Unless otherwise indicated, all Scripture quotations are taken from the Holy Bible,
New International Version®, NIV®. Copyright © 1973, 2011 by Biblica, Inc.™ Used
by permission of Zondervan. All rights reserved worldwide. www.zondervan.com.
Scripture quotations marked NKJV are taken from the New King James Version®.
Copyright © 1982 by Thomas Nelson, Inc. Used by permission. All rights reserved.

LCCN 2012954693
ISBN 978-0-7814-0867-7
eISBN 978-0-7814-0881-3

The Team: Don Pape, James Lund, Amy Konyndyk, Renada Arens, Karen Athen
Cover Design: Nick Lee
Cover Photos: Shutterstock, stock.xchng

Printed in the United States of America
First Edition 2013

1 2 3 4 5 6 7 8 9 10

113012

*"For it is because men have nothing 'high and lifted up' to raise their eyes to, nothing bigger than themselves and their own world to worship and wonder at, nothing more certain than their own ideas by which to steer their destiny, nothing more inspiring than their own goodness to lead them to repentance, that life grows stale, feverish and frustrated, and bad dreams become a matter of course."*

Unknown

*"Therefore, if anyone is in Christ, the new creation has come: The old has gone, the new is here!"*

2 Corinthians 5:17

# CONTENTS

# FOREWORD

"Are we there yet?"

Traveling across western states with my salesman dad, I spoke those words like many impatient eight-year-olds. Now, as a card-carrying member of the brotherhood of men, I confess that we don't like to stop to ask for directions. One husband responded to his wife's inquiry this way: "I don't know where we're going, but we're making great time!"

How's your road trip working out?

Perhaps you've got a lot of stuff but are running on empty. Or your 401(k) is on life support. You identify with a Cymbalta commercial, and your wife just told you that her life is like a Lifetime movie. Can your script be rewritten? Instead of focusing on shaving strokes off your golf score or fixating on "mediscare," those of us in our fifties and beyond must choose to "flourish like a palm tree … still bear[ing] fruit in old age" (Ps. 92:12–14).

Your departure toward newness begins now. This book will examine you more penetratingly than any TSA airport screening. Allow a layover. God has spared no expense in helping you know where you're going so that you'll know when you get there.

As Steve Silver's Florida pastor, I have watched his own New Man Journey. Years ago we prayed about how he could be a high-impact player in semiretirement and retirement years, knowing that it is never too late to head in the right direction. He was heart-deep in desiring a life change in men and would be a catalytic leader of large and small men's groups. In his new book, he challenges us to move from regular-guy status to active-duty special ops, embedded behind enemy lines.

At our church, many of our laity, like Steve, have stopped chasing the American Dream for the "vision from heaven" (Acts 26:19). Steve's sweet spot is connecting with guys who feel that talk about inwardness is like being the last kid picked in a "shirts and skins" game—and they're the "skins." Steve rejects Kipling's motto, "He travels the fastest who travels alone," calling for caring but challenging community.

This book hums with energy, grabbing you by your mental, spiritual, and emotional lapels. As a skilled word-weaver, Steve employs unforgettable growth-pictures: dragon caves, flowing rivers, updated computers, empty snake skins, acquired corporations, new houses, and healthy lawns.

Since women purchase 80 percent of Christian books, it could be that I am talking to a woman right now. Ladies, you have learned not to be a dripping faucet with your husband, but to be like the fizz of soda pop to a thirsty man. Tell him to read this foreword, dive into the book, and be impressed with the author's transparency, love for his wife, and her respect for him.

When I asked my dad, "Are we there yet?" he would smile and encourage me, "Look at the scenery, Hayes—enjoy the journey." So let's buckle up and move on. You'll enjoy this Journey.

After all, we're not There ... yet.

Dr. Hayes Wicker
Senior Pastor of First Baptist Church Naples

# ACKNOWLEDGMENTS

My wife, Sandy—for encouraging me to express in writing the passion and challenge that have driven me, and for being the anvil on which so much of my New Man metal has been forged. *1-4-3*

My children and grandchildren—for patiently coaxing out the best in me over the years with your constant love and all-too-often-needed grace.

Men's Golf Fellowship (MGF)—You are the pioneers. This book grew out of my love for and time with all of you these past ten years.

MGF Small Group—for your openness and mutual accountability on our journey together. I've learned more from you than I can express here.

Dan Woodbury—for initiating the idea for a book and cheerleading the whole way.

My friends at David C Cook—for taking a chance on this project and for your support and assistance along the way.

James Lund—for your insightful and constructive editorial support.

Dr. Hayes Wicker—whose foreword to the book speaks for itself to the great friend and encourager he's been.

All who so graciously provided work-in-progress and prepublication opinions, suggestions, and endorsements.

Stan Geyer (1948–2012)—for his friendship, partnership in MGF, encouragement of *New Man Journey* ... and for leading the way to ultimate victory.

# INTRODUCTION

If you're a retired guy—or are approaching retirement—or are simply thinking ahead to your senior years, then this book is for you. You may be in the sweet spot of life, reeling from a crisis, struggling with unforeseen issues, or somewhere in between. Whatever the case, my guess is that you've given life your all, have tried to make an impact as a husband, father, colleague, and friend, and are hoping for an even better endgame.

Only there's a problem.

You can't quite define it, but it gnaws at you. You're dissatisfied. You have questions: Will this tour through the years end the way you planned? Is each day filled with too much routine and too little substance? Is there more to life than this?

Are you missing something?

These are common questions, especially near the end of a career, after many years of marriage, or when the bloom is off the rose of retirement. I know the feeling because I've been there myself. It was questions like these that launched me on an amazing journey—one that placed me in the center of a movement of a thousand men in southwest Florida, guys who now meet weekly in small groups to discuss "meaning in retirement" challenges and opportunities.

This book has grown out of ten years of intimate conversations with many of these men. It addresses the prominent and growing concerns of those of us who sense, like the poet Andrew Marvell, "time's winged chariot hurrying near."[1] We can't reverse our body's aging process. There's no reason, however, for our spirit to remain stuck in a holding pattern. We're capable of much more. We can make the rest of our lives the best of our lives.

In the final chapter of his classic work *Mere Christianity*, C. S. Lewis provided a picture of what I'm talking about. He was not referring to someone who's only tinkered with a few adjustments, but to a person entirely transformed. He called it the "New Man":

> Already the new men are dotted here and there all over the earth. Some, as I have admitted, are still hardly recognisable: but others can be recognised. Every now and then one meets them. Their very voices and faces are different from ours: stronger, quieter, happier, more radiant. They begin where most of us leave off. They are, I say, recognisable; but you must know what to look for. They will not be very like the idea of 'religious people' which you have formed from your general reading. They do not draw attention to themselves. You tend to think you are being kind to them when they are really being kind to you. They love you more than other men do, but they need you less.... They will usually seem to have a lot of time: you will wonder where it comes from. When you have recognized one of them, you will recognize the next one much more easily.[2]

Does Lewis's description resonate with you? Have you ever met someone like this? You can be one of these people. There's a New Man inside each of us, eager to be reactivated after a time of neglect or simply waiting to be discovered and kicked into gear. What I'm proposing through this book is a journey of the spirit, a chance to press the refresh button of your life.

It's not too late. Your New Man is waiting for you, ready to be awakened. It's the best journey you'll ever take.

# NOTES

1. Andrew Marvell, "To his coy mistress," *Luminarium,* October 20, 1999, accessed October 11, 2012, http://www.luminarium.org/sevenlit/marvell/coy.htm.
2. C. S. Lewis, *Mere Christianity* (New York: Harper Collins, 2001), 223.

# 1

# LET'S GET REAL

To get our New Man Journey started in the right
direction, we've got to be honest with ourselves
about who we are and where we're going.

All journeys begin somewhere. Was there ever a time in your life
when you had the urge to just pick up and go? Try something completely new? Break the mold, shake it up, maybe even change your
life? Do you remember the excitement? The anticipation? Those great
feelings are usually the domain of youth, but they don't need to be.
As we get older, the circumstances of our lives may limit our physical explorations, but those inner longings have no such constraints.
These aspirations ignite journeys of the heart and spirit.

We're here at the beginning of what will be one of those journeys—one that will illuminate our understanding and challenge our views about how best to live the rest of our lives. That's a big statement. This is a big topic. Stay with me. The juice is worth the squeeze.

We're built to learn, change, and grow. To become who and what we were created to be. If we're not there yet, something inside stirs a longing for more, for something different. That's a good problem to have. I had it.

My need for a more purposeful life reached a crescendo ten years ago. At fifty-five, I'd achieved business success and financial stability. I was on good footing with my wife, family, friends, and faith. A comfortable early retirement was in sight. Life was good. Things were stable. I could finally relax and coast.

Yet something was wrong with that picture. It was incomplete. Had I finished one major phase of my life just to sit in an easy chair? I knew that dog wouldn't hunt. I needed more. More in my friendships. More in my marriage. More with my family. Most importantly, less of Steve and more of the Lord. Knowing I couldn't do this alone, I engaged others as sojourners on that quest and discovered that my needs and desires were the same as theirs.

Over the last ten years, these travelers and I have discovered two things that are essential for this journey: honesty and humility. These character cousins are the guardrails on our road. Without them, we'll lose our way. With them, we'll reach our destination. I'm excited to travel this road with you. Along the way, I'll disclose personal challenges that are a little uncomfortable to share. There are things I've had to admit to myself to make progress on my journey. I'll be asking you to be honest with yourself as well—to get real. I believe we're alike in many ways, so there won't be many surprises.

A few of the stories in the pages ahead are composites of the journeys of many men I've known. We'll see ourselves in them. Learn and grow with them. Let's begin with one about a former postal worker I'll call Gary and see how he's faring.

Gary's wife, Audrey, still wears her winter coat as she stands in the kitchen. She yanks open drawers and cabinets. "I don't know what to make for dinner," she says. "We're out of everything."

Gary sits at the kitchen table going through the mail. He's got his coat on too. It keeps the heat bills down.

"We could go out," he says.

Audrey knows better. "You know we can't afford that."

Gary feels his face redden. Is it his fault that the recession kicked in right after he took early retirement from the post office? That they'd drained the rest of their savings helping their kids get through community colleges? That now, not even the local grocery stores seem interested in hiring a sixty-year-old?

"I had an interview today," he snaps. "I'm doing the best I can."

Audrey turns away from the counter to look at him. "I know that."

He tosses a pile of bills onto the corner of the table and stands up. "Why can't you plan ahead? How hard is it to figure out a few meals for the week?"

Audrey's mouth opens, but for a few seconds nothing comes out.

"You know I'm helping out with the church auction," she finally says. "This is a crazy week for me. Don't you have time to help me just a little?"

*Don't I have time?* he thinks to himself. *Sure, I'm not working. I have all the time in the world!*

"Forget it," he says, his voice rising. "You don't have to make dinner for me. I'll get my own." With that, he stomps out of the room and the house, slamming the front door behind him.

A brisk breeze hits Gary in the face and instantly lowers his body temperature. The frigid air cools his anger as well. What's wrong with him anyway? Why is he so mad? He knows he shouldn't blame their problems on Audrey. Sure, he isn't too happy about needing to go back to work, or the fact that he's having so much trouble finding a job. But in many ways, life is good. They're both healthy, and the kids are doing fine. His daughter and son-in-law are even expecting their first child.

*So why does the future feel so bleak?*

Gary thought that by the time he was in his sixties, he'd have life pretty well figured out. He thought he'd have enough money set aside to live on and a loving family with whom to share his retirement years. Now that he's there, it's not quite what he expected. Disappointment. Emptiness. Confusion. Gary feels as if he's riding a train into a dark tunnel and isn't too sure he wants to know what's ahead.

A man named Tom is in a very different place ... yet not so different. His story is next.

*I don't understand.*

Tom eases the new, fully loaded, red Mercedes SL500 roadster out of the dealership and onto US Highway 1. Though it's a crisp October day, he has the top down. He can see the leaves turning in the maples alongside the road. He can also see his reflection in the mirror: the strong chin, the Louis Vuitton Evasion sunglasses, the full head of hair with some graying at the temples, a look some describe as "ruggedly handsome."

Tom feels eyes on him as he signals left. A blonde in a black BMW slows down and lets him change lanes for the turn onto Putnam Avenue. She takes a second glance as he makes the turn.

*I just don't get it.*

Tom had written a check for the full amount to buy the Mercedes, more than $130,000. He'd briefly negotiated on the price—he is a derivatives trader, after all—but the effort was only halfhearted. The point is that he no longer needs to haggle. After all these years, the eighteen-hour days and seemingly endless running of models and computations have finally paid off. Commissions, bonuses, and promotions have come his way. His credit cards are no longer issued by Kmart and Kohl's but by Neiman Marcus and Saks. The little home he and Brandy shared has been exchanged for a 6,500-square-foot estate—which doesn't include the pool house.

*It's not supposed to feel like this.*

Tom and Brandy are members of the most prestigious country club in Greenwich. They and their two kids summer on Nantucket and ski Breckenridge over the kids' winter breaks. Tom is fifty-five years old and, at last, everything is coming together the way it's supposed to. He's in position to enter early retirement and enjoy his golden years. The Mercedes is the final jewel in the crown, a symbol of all he's achieved and become.

*So why do I feel so empty?*

He steers onto Stonebridge Court, maneuvers past the manicured lawns and iron gates, and pulls into his driveway. His hands shake slightly as he presses the automatic garage door opener and aims for the middle space in the immaculate three-car garage. Even in the dim light, the Mercedes glows.

Tom turns off the engine and stares out the windshield for a full minute. Then he covers his face with his hands and begins to cry.

## DEFINING THE PROBLEM

Can you relate to Gary or Tom? Maybe you're a guy who, like Gary, has watched the recession or some other catastrophe chew up your well-laid retirement plans like a paper shredder. You're frustrated with your situation and sparring with your spouse—yet you sense deep down that the real problem is something quite different.

Maybe you click with Tom's story. You've been devoted to your career for decades. You've made fortunate financial choices and are now set up to enjoy the retired life. However, your meaning, identity, and security have gotten too wrapped up in your success, prestige, and nest egg. Something inside is telegraphing that this is hollow. That you may have missed an important turn along the way. That all is not well.

Or you may have been retired for a while now, but the daily rounds on the links and holiday visits with the children and grandchildren aren't quite as invigorating as you'd hoped. You feel as if you're making a farewell tour so that you can quietly step aside. You're missing the passion and purpose that your old job provided, but don't quite know how to fill it.

My story is a little like Tom's. I started out with nothing. Then I discovered I had a talent for problem solving, became a management consultant, and built a firm. I achieved success early and enjoyed the benefits that brings. Despite all that, I was insecure. When speaking with friends and colleagues, I dropped the names of my well-known clients and in other subtle (and not so subtle) ways conveyed that I was a "player," that I was important.

In other words, I was still operating too much out of what I call my Old Man—the self-focused attitudes and habits that were part of me from way back.

I've been working on this Old Man/New Man transformation since I gave my life to Jesus Christ forty-two years ago. I was a young man of twenty-three at the time. Before then, my life was my life, my goals were my goals, and my standards of personal excellence were loosely based on role models and my own sense of right and wrong.

That was enough to get by, but not a North Star—certainly nothing worth committing my life to.

Then, through an extraordinary set of circumstances and an evening dialogue with a beautiful young woman who would become my wife, Jesus stood before me and invited me to follow Him. I didn't hesitate. I'm glad I didn't. That late night is when the self-focused life I'd known took a backseat and the one I'm now living for Him became my purpose and passion. It's hard to imagine how the last forty-two years would have unfolded if the Lord's Word, friendship, and guiding presence had not been etched in my mind and on my heart.

Don't get me wrong; this hasn't been a walk in the park. The Old Man who controlled me BC (before Christ) and who I renounced way back then hasn't died an easy death. He still tries to backseat drive. Killing him off has been a hard-fought battle, because I'm a stubborn, willful guy. I've given up chunks of the old Steve over the years and known the freedom and release a man feels when he can at last put down a really heavy suitcase. But until five years ago, I still carried, not in my hands but on my back, a bear of a burden—money.

Starting in 2008 and continuing in 2009, my efforts at personal transformation were deeply challenged. Lehman Brothers collapsed and the S&P 500 was cut in half—as were thirty-five years of my retirement savings. Suddenly, I discovered how far I'd plunged. My physical security system was an ATM: Attachment to Money. My hope and sense of value depended on the size of my bank account far more than I'd realized. With that threatened, I felt exposed.

Yet I was right where I needed to be. My financial setback was one of the best things that ever happened to me. It was the explosive needed to blow apart my carefully crafted security shell, opening my mind, heart, and spirit to new possibilities. I was at the point in my life where I needed to slay the big dragon Mammon once and for all. I was finally ready to kick the decades of my New Man Journey into high gear.

I hope you're ready too.

# HOUSECLEANING

Years ago, I had a dream—or maybe it was a nightmare. In the dream, my house was a big, beautiful home on a street filled with other great homes. A few houses down the street was my second home, a little vacation house. This second house was much smaller than the others and didn't look like it belonged. I went inside. The paint on the walls was chipping and peeling. The ceilings were low, the floors crooked. The volumes on the bookshelves were mildewed and smelly. The furniture was in disrepair. The floors were stained. It wasn't pretty.

I went to the bathroom and flushed the toilet. To my horror, the water flowed over the rim and kept coming. Wastewater ran everywhere. The fluid was three inches deep in every room in the house before it stopped.

I looked around at the mess. I wanted to slap a Condemned sign on the front door and just walk away. However, I owned the house. I'd invested in it. I had an obligation to put it back in repair. The task seemed overwhelming and unpleasant, but I was resigned to take it on.

I scrubbed and mopped. Within minutes (remember, this was a dream), the water subsided and the floors returned to their dry but stained condition. I knew my first order of business was to address the septic issue. I went back into the bathroom with the intention of clearing the blockage causing the backup. Next to the toilet was a small manhole cover, which seemed like a good place to start.

When I slowly lifted the cover, I was horrified. Solid waste proceeded to pour out of the hole onto the floor. I slammed the cover back down. My problem was much bigger than I'd thought.

Mercifully, that was when I woke up. I was back in my real home—clean, organized, and in perfectly good working condition. What a relief that I didn't have to deal with that awful septic mess!

Or did I?

Dream interpreters say the house in your dreams represents your life. Ugh. If that contaminated house was my life, I was in serious trouble. Of course, this was just a second home, one I apparently didn't frequent too often. Yet it was still mine. Maybe I had some work to do after all.

Why am I sharing this most unpleasant of personal dreams? Because I believe we all have some version of that toxic house. It's a part of our life that, though out of sight and out of mind, is in need of maintenance, maybe even pumping and flushing. You may say, "Hey, don't project your septic problems on me!" And you might be justified. You may be flushed clean and pure, with fresh springs running from the top of your head to the bottom of your feet. If you suspect, however, that you may be among the unflushed, please read on.

Retirement is great. No doubt about it. Travel. Golf. Fishing. More time with your wife, children, grandchildren, and friends. But what if that's not enough? What if we could have something more powerful, more effective, more permanent, and even more fulfilling? What if getting to those required some preliminary assessment and investigation? Would we be satisfied with throwing a couple quarts of Drano into our version of the septic monster? Would we be okay with straightening up a bit, dusting off the books, throwing on a new coat of paint, and applying a dose of Glade to mask the odor?

While that's easier than professional cleanup and renovation, we both know we wouldn't be satisfied if our house was in that condition. If there's a chance your inner life needs housecleaning, you have the time and inclination in your retirement years to undertake the project, and you have a good contractor lined up for the work, are you willing to make the investment?

If your answer is "Yes" or even "Maybe," you're in the right place.

## WHAT DO YOU DO?

I wish you could join me at a place called the Front Porch Cafe in Putney, Vermont. Imagine a quintessentially quaint and cool town of sixteen hundred residents. Now, add a little main street with a general store, town hall, library, volunteer fire house, post office, book and gift shop, art gallery, pizzeria, public vegetable garden, co-op grocery store, church, and, of course, my beloved Front Porch Cafe, where great ideas are discussed and most of the world's problems get resolved. I love Putney, especially the little perch from which I can see the comings and goings of the town in summer and enjoy a great big fire in an overstuffed chair around the holidays in the winter.

This place is one of the great joys of my semiretirement life. I bring friends here every chance I get. It's a place where time stops, the soul takes a deep breath, and the problems of life are temporarily as far away as the thirties and forties music playing on the stereo.

Maybe what I love most about Putney is that everyone is content to just be themselves. No one wastes time trying to impress the people around them.

That's not how it is in most other places I've been. Back in the land of male bonding, whether we're talking about guys who are still in the game, are semiretired like me, or are fully embracing the golden years, it's a different dynamic. If your world is anything like mine, when I meet another guy, the questions go something like this: "Hi, where are you from? How long have you been here? What brought you here? Where do you live? Tell me about your family. Are you still working? What do (or did) you do?"

Isn't that last question what the others really lead up to? We all know where the preamble is headed. Sure, we want to know the other stuff, but what you do or did helps me define you. It tells me about your station in life and your jumping-off point into retirement. For competitive guys like me—and isn't that pretty much all of us?—it allows me to establish where you and I stand in the pecking order.

Maybe this helps explain why so many of us "fudge" our answers and exaggerate our achievements. Does our old job as a midlevel manager suddenly turn into a vice president's position? Do we take a little more credit for that merger than we really deserve? For that matter, in conversation, does our golf average somehow drop from the low nineties into the mideighties or our bowling score rise from 173 to 195?

My point is that we guys are not always honest with each other. We hold back from each other the things that are real, that allow someone to look under the hood. But by holding back, we prevent the mutual discoveries that we so need to make genuine connections.

This is why, in the few instances when someone asks me where I went to high school, I take pleasure in telling them I was expelled in my sophomore year. For about three months, I was the ringleader of a group of thirty or so students who skipped school, danced, drank, and generally raised a ruckus. This information is usually a conversation stopper, which is a beautiful thing. It shatters the expectation of what get-acquainted conversation is all about. For me, it's freeing and authentic. For that one moment, at least, the connection level is elevated.

## LIVING BY DIFFERENT RULES

Lying is a bad idea no matter how you try to justify it. But the exaggerations and partial truths we tell others are inconsequential compared to the deceptions we might be telling ourselves. Our retirement plan may be to eat well, exercise, invest prudently, give proper attention to church obligations, and live for the day. We say to ourselves that this is enough, that we have all we need and are meant to have.

Yet there is that nagging little voice in the back of our minds. It could be whispering about loss of passion and purpose, deteriorating marriage and family relationships, superficial friendships, frustrations with declining stature, influence, and finances. Perhaps we're telling that voice that we've got everything under control. Maybe we're stifling it. Can you relate to what I'm saying? How about it? Have you been totally honest with yourself about who you are and how you're doing? Is it possible that something vital is missing from your life? Getting close to the nerve center is mission-critical to discovering just what that missing piece is—and what to do about it.

Are you ready to let your guard down and experience that part of yourself that has no age, that isn't trapped and bound by a deteriorating body? The nagging voice inside could be your New Man, waiting to be discovered and released.

The New Man sees everything with a different set of eyes. He is virtually free from fear and anxiety because he lives by different rules. Financial security, worldly success, status, and physical health are no longer the pillars on which his life stands. He strives not for personal gain but for the prize of continual transformation. His desire is for as many as possible to move toward that same prize.

The New Man isn't "happy" in the way that a bite of chocolate provides temporary pleasure. Instead, he is joy-filled and humble. He is a man who knows his former lower nature and is always amazed and thankful for the forgiveness he's received and the progress he's made. He sees others as vulnerable and in need of the grace he himself receives. He understands and passionately embraces the chance to consistently and generously sow seeds of God's love, hope, and transforming power into hearts.

As we explore these ideas in the chapters to come, I urge you to be authentic. Your honesty can serve as the dynamite for blowing away those encrustations that keep you trapped. The entrance to an entirely fresh inner life, the New Man I'm talking about, is just ahead.

Let's continue.

# 2

# WHAT I DON'T KNOW WON'T HURT ME

**We're afraid of what we'll find if we look at ourselves too closely, yet the reward is worth the risk.**

In the movie *City Slickers*, Mitch Robbins (a radio ad salesman played by Billy Crystal) tries opening up to his boss, Lou, over lunch. It's Mitch's thirty-ninth birthday, and he's feeling disappointed with his life: "Did you ever reach a point in your life, where you say to yourself: 'This is the best I'm ever going to look, the best I'm ever going to feel, the best I'm ever going to do,' and it ain't that great?" Lou responds with, "Happy birthday."[1]

Not exactly empathetic, but fairly typical of the sensitivity level of most guys. We're not all that good in such situations, especially with other men. Contemplating and sharing our feelings just feels awkward.

Just what is it with us guys? Why do we consider soul-searching and opening up to be the purview of women and those other guys—the *sensitive* ones? Why do we poke fun at the notion of sharing groups, cringe at the idea of disclosing our inner feelings, and joke with each other about bonding? Why do men relate to each other predominantly with levity, humor, and personal digs? Why do we try so hard to keep it light? Have you ever thought about this? Is it just the way we are? Men are from Mars, women are from Venus. Is that a sufficient explanation?

Don't get me wrong. I enjoy the light side of guy-relating as much as anyone and contribute my fair share to maintaining a safe distance from most of my male friends. But let me ask: Do you ever find yourself wishing you could linger a bit longer to talk about other things? Things besides sports, politics, markets, business, family, movies, books, health, and the trials and tribulations of mutual acquaintances? Is there anything wrong with that need? Is there someone in your life with whom you can do that? Have you ever tried?

Here's the problem: we guys essentially don't give ourselves permission to go deep with anyone—not our wives, not our children, certainly not our friends, and really not even ourselves. Why is this? Let's explore it, beginning with our wives.

# I CAN'T EVEN TALK TO MY WIFE

Assuming you're married, how long has it been? Chances are a long time. In fact, your wife may have given you this book in hopes of advancing you personally and spiritually. Regardless, what do you discuss when you're alone? Let me guess. The children and grandchildren. The latest news. Political candidates. What's for dinner. Scheduled activities. What each of you did today. What you're doing tonight. Future dates. Obligations. So-and-so's health, death, or problems. Your upcoming trip. The weather here or where your families live. The book you're reading. The movie you just saw. Your yard. Your pool. Your dog. The neighbor's dog. The meaning of life.

*Wait* ... how did that get in there? Sorry. Which Medicare supplement plan to go with. What to do for Thanksgiving and Christmas this year. Whether to have the deck stained this spring or to give it another year. Whether you love each other as much as you did when you first fell in love.

*Oops*, I did it again. That last one has a different feel than the others, doesn't it? It belongs with questions like these: Is there anything you need that you haven't been getting from me? If you could change anything about me, what would that be? Do we harbor any feelings of resentment or disappointment toward each other? Have we forgiven each other for all the harsh words, rude behavior, and disrespect we've imposed over the years? What are our mutual hopes and dreams for the future? Are these still possible? What's missing in our relationship? Is it too late to find and put in those missing pieces? How should we go about that? Are we taking interest in and encouraging one another? Are we still in love? Are we growing old well together? Are we being shining examples of love and rocks of strength for our family and close friends?

*Hmm.* Does this set of questions make you nervous? Can you envision yourself changing the conversation to include these along with other necessary, pedestrian subjects? How would your wife react? Would these questions make her uncomfortable? Would she rebuff them? Would she think you were crazy? If you told her you were serious, would she give the questions a chance? If so, where would they lead? Would she be prepared for the answers? Would you? Or is all this better left covered over and unexplored?

This reminds me of a funny scene in the Woody Allen movie *Annie Hall.* Alvy Singer (played by Woody) is having imaginary conversations with strangers on the street about their relationships. He stops a young, trendy-looking couple, arms wrapped around each other, and asks them to account for their happiness. "I'm very shallow and empty," the young woman says, "and I have no ideas and nothing interesting to say." Her companion chimes in: "And I'm exactly the same way."[2]

Seriously, though, how you answer the questions above may tell a lot about your willingness and preparedness for healthy self-examination. Why? Because the kinds of questions I'm raising require deeper-than-typical levels of honesty, humility, and reverence. We're not accustomed to having and are likely not prepared for conversations like these. Most of us couldn't pass the red-face test if we had to describe the true nature of our relationship with our wives.

Consider the story of Ray and Birgit. They met thirty-eight years ago. He was a USAF Airman First Class at the Joint Warfare Center in Jatta, Norway, and she was a teacher at the International School in nearby Stavanger. They fell in love and were married a year later in a small wedding in Birgit's Evangelical Lutheran family church. Two years and one child later, Ray and Birgit relocated to Edwards Air Force Base in Southern California. After achieving the rank of Technical Sergeant, Ray left the air force for an opportunity as an assistant program manager with a private aerospace company in San Bernardino. That was the beginning of a great career spanning the next thirty years.

When Ray was fifty-seven, he took early retirement. By then they had three grown children, two of them married, and four grand-children, all living within 150 miles of their Redlands stucco home. Ray and Birgit's whole lives had been dedicated to work and family. They'd rarely taken vacations together. When they were finally empty nesters, they filled most of their free time with the routine of visiting their children's families, tending to household obligations, and going out with friends.

It finally dawned on them: it was Ray and Birgit's turn to live for themselves. They charted out all the places they'd go, interests they'd take up, and old acquaintances with whom they'd reconnect. They became excited about their newfound freedom and the possibilities of rediscovering the joys of earlier years together. For two years, all went well. They were so active that they were even harder to keep track of than when Ray worked. They were in good health, enjoyed their activities, and were relatively free from financial concerns due to savings and a good pension.

As they settled into their third year, however, some of the excitement faded. Ray and Birgit began to realize that their lives couldn't be one big playground whirlwind. It was time to consider the rest of their years in more practical terms. Where would they live? What would they do to be productive? What would their new "normal" be?

Ray sits at the kitchen table, the newspaper spread out before him. Birgit is across from him, sipping from a mug of coffee. "So," he begins, "where do you want to be in five years? Here in this house? A smaller house in Redlands? Someplace else altogether?"

Birgit shrugs her shoulders. "I still want to be able to see the kids and grandkids, you know that," she says. "But besides that, I don't know. I have a hard enough time deciding what to do for the next week, let alone five years."

As Ray listens to Birgit, his mind lights on a disturbing new thought. *Will our marriage be status quo for the next five years? We used to be closer. Will these plans get us back in touch?*

He realizes they've grown apart during their work and family-raising years. *Was what we experienced the past two years just the exuberance of our new environment, not the love of our youth?*

Ray doesn't dare verbalize this, but he knows and feels it. He resolves to map out a strategy for the years ahead. Yet he fears this won't be enough to revitalize their marriage. *When,* he wonders, *did we lose what we had? When did life catch us off guard and rob us of our intimacy? How can we retrace and renew our life together?*

Can you relate to Ray? If you're married and were asked to write a condensed history of your relationship, what would that look like? When did the passion change? When did the glances from across the crowded room stop? Do you find yourself looking for other things to occupy your time to avoid one-on-one time with your wife? Do you prefer time with others? Is it easier to talk to friends than to her? If you think these tough questions don't apply to you, try bringing this book to her right now and reading them together. Ask her if they're relevant. Ask her to be honest. Tell her you're serious.

Are you willing to do this? If not, why? If you believe your communications are deep, intimate, and healthy, you have nothing to lose.

Tell the truth. You both want and can have more. This can begin now. This is the first and most important step in your New Man Journey, a step that engages your life partner and closest friend in the process. By the way, you're not alone in this. The only difference between you and 90 percent of other guys who've been married this long is your willingness to take this step. Once you do it, here's what you're likely to find:

- You've drifted further apart than you knew.
- She is less fulfilled by you than you thought.
- The embers of love and interest that brought you together in the first place are still alive.

- There's more potential for meaning in this relationship than you hoped.
- She is more willing to forgive, forget, and start over than you expected.
- She needs the real you more than you knew.

## OPENING UP

Ray and Birgit ended up moving to a new home in a San Diego golfing community, where they've been living for the past year. The transition from Redlands was a good distraction, but nothing in their relationship really changed. Ray decided to take the risk of opening up to Birgit about his feelings. He chose dinner at the country club as the setting. Let's see how it goes.

"Birgit, are you happy with all this?" Ray gestures with his hand around the room.

"What do you mean?" she says.

"I mean, are you satisfied with our retirement?"

Birgit folds her napkin in her lap. "Let's just say … I'm still adjusting. We've only been here a year. I like our house. I enjoy the new friends we're making. I wish my golf game was better." They both laugh. "Why are you asking? What's on your mind?"

"It's hard to say, exactly. I agree with you about our house and the people here. That's all great. But I'm having trouble adjusting. I'm not sure all this is working for me."

"All this? Isn't this what we've always wanted and planned for? To relax, try new things, spend more time together?"

Ray nods. "Yes, definitely. This is exactly what we envisioned. It's just that … well, simply that … now that we're here, it's not what I thought it would be. Something's missing."

"What's missing? Work? Your business travel? Our old neighborhood and routine? Those are the only things that have changed."

"No, I don't think I'd want those back," Ray says. "Though work did fill a void."

"I think that's natural," Birgit says. "Your career was a huge part of your life. Leaving that left a hole that can't get filled overnight. Just be patient. You'll find many interests and projects to replace your work life."

Ray takes a deep breath. "I'm sure you're right about that," he says, "but there's more to it."

"More?" Ray reaches across the table for Birgit's hand. She starts to put it out, then pulls it back. "What are you saying?"

Ray looks at her, not sure how to put his thoughts into words. "I guess I'm saying that something's missing … with us."

Birgit puts her hand to her head. For a moment, Ray fears she might pass out. He reaches again for her hand. Birgit suddenly stands.

"I'm sorry," she says. "This isn't happening. I have to leave. Please get the check. I'm going to the ladies' room. Just go home. Leave the car."

She stumbles, and Ray leaps up to help her. She pulls her arm away. "I'm fine. Just get the check. Walk home. We'll discuss this later."

People dining smile politely as Birgit leaves the room. They look over at Ray and talk in hushed voices. Ray feels totally alone. Embarrassed. Ashamed. Hurt and concerned for Birgit. He realizes he's just made a huge mistake, yet he's relieved his feelings are out.

Birgit isn't home when Ray gets there on foot. It's now eight thirty. His heart sinks. *She's never done anything like this before. Then again, I've never said anything to challenge or threaten our marriage or my love for her. What have I done? What an idiot. What was I thinking? There's no easy way out of this. What should I do?*

Ray's mind races through his options. *I'll backtrack. All I said was there's something missing with us. Not such a big deal. I'll minimize what's missing. Make it easy. But that's not true. There's something big missing. Has been for a long time. Maybe always. We share a life together but aren't really close. Hardly ever discuss anything other than family and routine. Never had all that much in common. Is this the way it is with most couples after a while? Does romance and excitement just fade? Wind down? Run dry? Are any of our friends different?*

Ray thinks about couples they've known a long time. Most seem just like them. Taking each other for granted. Stapled together through life by children, grandchildren, finances, and logistics. Not much excitement. Some have more active social lives than he and Birgit. More friends. Travel more. But love each other more? Enjoy each other's company more? Have more physical attraction? Ray doesn't see it. He tries to resolve himself to the inevitability of all aging marriages. *We're fine. No worse off than most couples our age, and better than many.*

He hears the garage door open. Tenses. *This won't be easy.* Ray waits on the family room couch.

Birgit enters, tosses her keys on the kitchen counter, and walks past him. "I'm going to bed," she says. "Please sleep in the guest room."

Ray gets up. "Wait a minute, honey. You misunderstood. Everything's fine. I'm sorry for being so stupid. For hurting you. Let's talk. Please."

Birgit's expression is hard. Distant. Her eyes red and swollen. "I didn't misunderstand," she says. "I've known for a while. Oh, by the way, you're not the only one." She speaks with a controlled rage he hasn't seen, looking at him with daggers. "You're not the only one ... *missing* something! Everything's *not* fine!" She walks into the bedroom and slams the door.

Ray hears the door lock click. Knows, with that click, that their life together won't be the same. The door to their marriage as they've known it has just closed. He feels his blood draining out. He's alone in the family room of a new house with an unclear future.

The little bird clock in the kitchen chirps nine times. *I surprised her with that clock the day we moved in. She loved it.*

*Told me how happy she was here and how wonderful it would be. Now this. I want that day back.*

Ray goes to the bedroom door, intending to knock. He wants to make everything the way it was before he opened his mouth at dinner. He decides against it. He goes back to the family room. Lies down on the couch. Looks around the room. Searches for an answer.

*What should I do? I can't live without her, nor her without me. We're in this together. Can't go on the way we have been. Can't settle. Don't care if others do. What should I do? I'm stuck.* He decides to pray. *Hey, God ... if You're out there, I could use some help here.*

Okay, that didn't go so well. I didn't say it would always be easy. And Ray could have done a better job of opening up about his feelings and establishing a constructive dialogue. I don't know about you, but I've blown it on the wife-communications front more times than I can count. But I keep on trying and have, on balance, had more success than failure in this department. Although, I admit it, situations like Ray's are pretty tough. Hang in there. It gets better for him and Birgit later on.

So, if we're analyzing barriers to healthy self-examination, why did we start with marriage? Couldn't we have chosen something easier? I suppose we could have, but this is the mother lode. It's hard to lie here. Your highest, best qualities and deepest, darkest deceptions are wrapped around this relationship. When we set the first stick of dynamite here, we gain true access to the New Man Journey. Can we continue without this step? Sure. Can we set the dynamite and be prepared to light the fuse at some later point in this journey? Absolutely. But sooner or later, it has to happen.

Then again, you may be single. If you're divorced, widowed, or have never been married, this book is still for you. It's for anyone seeking more substantive relationships with those closest to him. For the guy with a desire to explore, discover, and become one of those New Men to whom C. S. Lewis referred. For the man willing to face and knock down the barriers along the way.

Let's look at another one of those big barriers.

## IF I LOOK INSIDE, I'M NOT SURE I'LL LIKE WHAT I SEE

What's your self-image? Self-image is "the idea one has of one's abilities, appearance, and personality." What do you believe people think about you? Which of the following key words would they use to describe you?

| | | |
|---|---|---|
| ☐ Tough | ☐ Funny | ☐ Demanding |
| ☐ Easygoing | ☐ Open | ☐ Closed |
| ☐ Friendly | ☐ Loose | ☐ Rigid |
| ☐ Wired | ☐ Relaxed | ☐ Compassionate |
| ☐ Hard-hearted | ☐ Relentless | ☐ Stubborn |
| ☐ Determined | ☐ Conforming | ☐ Eccentric |
| ☐ Conservative | ☐ Quiet | ☐ Gregarious |
| ☐ Introverted | ☐ Outgoing | ☐ Loner |
| ☐ People Person | ☐ Deep | ☐ Complicated |
| ☐ Simple | ☐ Blunt | ☐ Sarcastic |

| | | |
|---|---|---|
| ☐ Insincere | ☐ Truthful | ☐ Diplomatic |
| ☐ Leader | ☐ Follower | ☐ Charismatic |
| ☐ Low Profile | ☐ Respectful | ☐ Irreverent |
| ☐ Honest | ☐ Deceptive | ☐ Trustworthy |
| ☐ Fair | ☐ Selfish | ☐ Unselfish |
| ☐ Stingy | ☐ Generous | ☐ Extravagant |

What would you add to this list? Do you find this to be an easy exercise? I'll bet you don't. And why not? Because you're not exactly sure. You have impressions of what others might think, but those may or may not align with what you think about yourself. You may project a facade to the outside world different from the real you. On the other hand, your inside and outside attributes may be mirror images. Do you really know? Have you ever considered this? Does it matter? Does this smack of self-absorption?

It does to me, too, but here's the deal. Whether or not we admit it, most of us care a lot about how others view us. We consciously and unconsciously work hard at ensuring that others view us favorably.

Humor me a little. If others view you as stingy but you view yourself as generous, would that bother you? Would you want to know the reason for the misalignment? Pick another. Suppose others view you as cold but you view yourself as warm. Fake versus genuine. Caustic versus kind. Would any of these be a problem for you? Would you care? Of course you would. You'd care because you want to be the best man you can possibly be within the framework of your natural personality.

So, if others see you in ways you consider unfavorable, that's bound to bother you. Most of us, however, don't obsess about how others view us and (mercifully) don't see what they see. Imagine how hard it would be to go through life being able to read other people's thoughts and impressions about us.

Remember the movie *What Women Want?* Nick Marshall, a bachelor ad executive played by Mel Gibson, has a freak accident. An electrical shock in the bathtub leaves him with the uncanny ability to hear the thoughts of all women he encounters—even a female French poodle. Until this temporary anomaly, Nick considers himself God's gift to women. Then he learns the truth.

The morning after his accident, Nick encounters two female coworkers in the hallway at the office.

"Good mor—" Nick starts to say, but then he hears the first woman's thoughts: *Don't look up. He'll make me hear another disgusting joke. He's such a schmuck.*

Nick can't believe it. *She thinks I'm a schmuck?*

Then he hears the second woman's thoughts as she passes by: *Whoa, lighten up on that aftershave, buddy.*[3]

Nick's self-image is dealt an unwelcome blow.

How about it? Would you be surprised if you could see or hear others' opinions about you? Pleased? Mortified? Embarrassed? Would it drive you to serious self-examination and change? I wonder. The point is, most of us want what's best within us to be the person who engages our world. We might be unpleasantly surprised to find out that what we consider our best is not very impressive. We'd just as soon not know what we don't know. So, we avoid self-evaluation.

## I'M NOT ONE TO BARE MY SOUL

You're a regular guy. Your friends are regular guys. Regular guys keep their issues to themselves. This is written in the Regular Guy Handbook. As we already discussed, certain things are taboo in the world of "real men," and soul baring is at the top of that list. However, we might from time to time need someone to talk to about our problems. We're not necessarily in the habit of discussing these with our wives, nor are we sure we can tell them everything. So what do we do with this apparent conflict?

We can start by blowing through the taboo. Who invented this anyway? John Wayne? Audie Murphy? Knute Rockne? George Patton? Steven Seagal? Vince Lombardi? The Terminator? Vito Corleone? Your father? Maybe it's a composite of these and a million other individuals, characters, and myths embedded in the male psyche.

In *The Godfather*, crooner Johnny Fontane (played by Al Martino) goes to Vito Corleone (played by Marlon Brando) to ask for help in obtaining a movie part. Johnny covers his face in his hands and begins to cry, saying, "I don't know what to do." The Godfather responds by slapping Johnny across the face and saying, "You can act like a man! What's the matter with you?"[4]

You get the point. The male stereotype is to be a brave, strong, unrelenting individual. Not much room for soul baring in the stereotype. And we actually buy into this.

Do you suppose Vito would have slapped Jesus of Nazareth around when He wept? Yes, Jesus wept. He wept at learning of the death of His friend Lazarus (John 11:35) and over the impending fate of His beloved Jerusalem (Luke 19:41). In Gethsemane on the night he was arrested, He labored in prayer so much that His sweat was like drops of blood (Luke 22:44), and He felt such anguish on the cross that He cried out, "My God, my God, why have you forsaken me?" (Matt. 27:46). And I'm sure our "man of suffering" (Isa. 53:3) wept many other times as He poured out His heart and soul to those who loved and followed Him, as well as those who despised, rejected, tortured, and killed Him.

I'll take my example from Jesus rather than Vito. How about you? You don't need to look any further than Saint Francis of Assisi, King David, and Jacob's son Joseph for other examples of great men who were not afraid to be led by their emotions from time to time. Here's what Chuck Swindoll has to say in reflection on the Genesis 43:24–30 account of Joseph's reunion with his brothers:

> Like the rest of us, great men and women encounter those times in life when they can no longer restrain their emotions. Composure flies away, and feelings take control. That was what happened to Joseph at this long-awaited moment in time. It is at such sacred crossroads words fail us. Often we need to get alone to gain our composure. Joseph did....
>
> Can't you imagine the scene? All of a sudden, the handsome, confident leader of millions has rushed to his bedroom and collapsed in sobs. All those years passed in review. All the loneliness. All the loss. All the seasons and birthdays and significant occasions without his family. It was too much to contain, like a rushing river pouring into a lake, swelling above the dam. His tears ran, and he

heaved with great sobs. All of a sudden, he was a little boy again, missing his daddy.

There have been times in my own life when I've had doubts, when I've stumbled over great cracks that appeared in my world. I've had those times when I climbed into my own bed and wept, crying out to God, just as you have. Such is life, especially when you decide to be real rather than protect some kind of super-confident image.[5]

Am I recommending we join a sensitivity group and start blubbering out all our pent-up feelings and emotions? Of course not. The point of this discussion is that we have permission. Permission to be open and honest with close male friends, wives, family members, priests, pastors, advisors, counselors, and others in our confidence. Not only do we have permission, but it is a requirement to enter into relationships of mutual honesty, support, and encouragement. If this sounds a little foreign but makes sense, you are ready. However, you may not know where or how to begin. Let's address that.

# I HAVE ZERO EXPERIENCE WITH THIS SORT OF THING

Have you noticed that the older you get, the less comfortable you are with unfamiliar things? There is so much you do well, routines you know, well-worn grooves you are able to navigate with little extra effort. Why bother with new challenges like a New Man Journey? I could provide all the pat answers but will let the experience of a real-life good friend (I'll call him Ernie) illustrate.

Ernie is one of those guys everyone wants to hang out with. He's straightforward, sincere, predictable, and easygoing. He also has a beautiful and consistent golf swing and is one of the better players in his club. Nothing erratic about his game or his life. He's simply a great combination of self-discipline, stability, humility, sincerity, graciousness, and interest in others.

Maybe a lot like you or some of the guys you know and most admire. He has a strong marriage to a good woman, a family that loves and respects him, a nice little business, and enough for a comfortable retirement. In short, he's navigated and carved out a good life for himself and enhanced the lives of those around him.

So what more could a guy like this possibly need? What would compel him to go looking for some missing part? It's not as if he didn't have religion and was searching for an answer to the meaning of life. All was well in that area too. In fact, all was nearly perfect. Nearly.

You might say that I was part of the "problem." I began Men's Golf Fellowship (MGF) ten years ago. This has grown into a gathering of men with a wide range of beliefs and faiths. We meet weekly for breakfast with guest speakers who talk about the application of their faith to their personal and professional lives. Many of us also meet in small groups in our golf clubs to discuss the "God and Life" issues facing us at this stage. I invited Ernie to one of our breakfasts a few years ago, and then to our discussion group. Here's what happened to him, in his own words:

When Steve was getting the Men's Golf Fellowship (MGF) groups started ten years ago, he invited me to participate, and I declined. At the time, I saw Steve as a little too "evangelical" for me. I was uncomfortable. I remember talking with him about it. I told him I wasn't that comfortable talking about my faith—that the way I was brought up, faith was more private and personal. I didn't want to be pushed. So, I sat out the first three or four years. Then I began to see that MGF was a great resource for understanding and growing my faith. I got involved and haven't looked back.

One of the MGF speakers, early on in my involvement, spoke about his faith development, and his story resonated with me completely. He was a business guy, and as such he had to make business decisions on a daily basis, evaluating courses of action. His approach in making decisions was logical and rational. He would get all the facts, research and study the situation, evaluate the risks, and weigh the pros and cons. His intuition played a part too, but only after a thorough analysis. Then he would make a decision, the best he could. He knew there was a possibility of being wrong but had to make a decision, since making no decision was a decision too. He said he saw no reason not to apply this same process to the question of faith.

To be a believer or not to be a believer? That is the question. Our MGF speaker felt he needed to answer that question. It might be the most important one he would ask in his lifetime. The consequences of not asking or answering it incorrectly could be quite severe—for eternity. He felt that not addressing it was irresponsible.

Why leave this to chance? No decision is a decision not to believe.

This reasoning made sense to me. It is the way a businessman thinks. I had been feeling a need to grow in faith for some years. I was raised and baptized a Christian, but my faith was pretty casual, informal, and generic. I believed in God, but in a general way. My faith felt incomplete ... like there was more ... like I was missing something. Maybe it was time for me to address this question of faith more directly and make a decision. To put my stake in the ground, so to speak. So this is what I set out to do.

I had finished reading the Bible by this time, and over the next several months applied myself to this question. In our MGF discussion group, we were reading the C. S. Lewis series of books on how he came to faith, and this reading helped clarify and bring it together for me. There is much that went into my considering this question. Daily prayer was part of it. But it was not something I agonized over.

Then, after a couple of false starts last year, I finally got up the courage to lead a discussion in our small group. The topic that I chose was "What does it mean to have a personal relationship with Jesus Christ?" This was when I really started to get it.

Until then, statements like "being born again," "giving yourself to Christ," "accepting Jesus Christ as your Lord and Savior," and "having a personal relationship with Jesus Christ" were foreign to me (or else I missed them in my childhood Christian upbringing). They were too personal and a little scary, and suggested "giving up control" and "not being in charge myself," which were things I held dear.

Then I realized, partly through leading that study, that being a Christian wasn't just believing in God and going to church. It was all those things that were foreign and scary to me: giving myself up to the Lord and having a personal relationship with Him ... giving up my pride, really changing my priorities in life, and becoming a new person.

Some people come to faith with the suddenness of a flash of light. This was my brother's and wife's experience. Several men in our MGF small group became believers that way. I think, in some ways, these are the lucky ones. Their experience is so strong and powerful, there is no room for doubt. For the rest of us it is different. We have to work at it, grind it out, pray and feel our way to faith. And, ultimately, we need to make the decision.

My decision did not feel like a "leap of faith." It felt like the logical conclusion to applying myself to the question of faith. I sought an answer, and the answer was there. For me the case for God is compelling and the case for Christianity is just as compelling. The theology and the empirical evidence that I have explored satisfy me completely.

Ernie certainly could have stayed in his groove. No one would have accused him of being ignorant about faith or ignoring this part of his life if he hadn't chosen to dig deeper through small group and individual discussions, read the Bible, and "grind out" the answers, as he put it. But something inside told him that wasn't enough. That this was important enough to explore. By taking that initiative, he made a discovery, which revealed that the "perfection" of his life up to that point paled in comparison to the *fullness* in store for his future.

## TAKE A LITTLE RISK

Some guys figure they get all they need on this topic from church or self-help books. So did Ernie. As I mentioned, he's one of the most self-disciplined guys I know. He was indeed progressing comfortably, personally and spiritually, on his former glide path. Then something happened. This was different. More urgent. More compelling. This got his attention. It was almost as if God grabbed him by the shoulders and spoke into his heart, "Ernie, you have a solid shot here, don't delay and possibly lose it." As Ernie put it, "The consequences of not asking [the question] or answering it incorrectly could be quite severe—for eternity." Those are not everyday stakes.

Until God intervened, going to church and reading personal development books were honest expressions of Ernie's search for answers. They were also somewhat safe. Not accompanied by the evangelical terminology that threatened his control. No "life-changing decision" necessary. Remember Ernie's first reaction to me? "A little too evangelical." I made him uncomfortable.

What was that discomfort? I believe Ernie was nervous about the implications of getting too close to what I represented. Someone who took his spiritual life too seriously. Perhaps a little extreme. I'd conjecture that, in Ernie's mind, spiritual life was 25 percent of a well-balanced diet of faith, family, work, and recreation. He probably thought along these lines: *People don't normally talk about Jesus at the golf club or other secular venues. Everything in its place and a place for everything. I'll respect your privacy, and you respect mine.*

Is this you? Do you find yourself agreeing with this stance? Ernie certainly did. He would have been right there a few years ago. So what happened to good old *normal* Ernie? Was he hit by a stray golf ball? Was he unwittingly wooed into a cult? Did he have a middle-of-the-night vision of hell that scared him into submission?

None of these. What happened was that he saw hundreds of men attending weekly breakfasts in his golf club, listening to other *normal* men talk about their faith—about when and how God became more real and important in their lives. This, coupled with the growing feeling that his faith was incomplete, drove him to his first MGF breakfast and the speaker's talk he described. That out-of-the-box experience stimulated the questioning that subsequently led to his decision.

That decision, according to Ernie's wife, has resulted in his becoming more compassionate and less compulsive. More self-aware and considerate. More appreciative of her and of life in general. More willing to, for example, visit an old friend in a nursing home. Ernie's wife also says that his faith journey has changed *their* relationship: "We communicate better. Our love is deeper, richer, and more meaningful."

If you can relate to Ernie's situation and experience even a little, I'd encourage you to find a different context for your own search. Don't stop going to church or reading, but break up the paradigm. Step into new territory. Expect the unexpected. In short, take a risk. Ernie did, and the results speak for themselves.

Am I suggesting you need to leave the comfort of your current life and go to the mission field to have a serious faith breakthrough? You know I'm not. Am I proposing you reengineer yourself to the point of being unrecognizable to your family and friends? You couldn't if you tried, and the outcome would be strained and inauthentic.

My proposition is much simpler. Ask God if you are indeed in balance in your spiritual life. Invite Him to take you somewhere that might be a little uncomfortable to get your attention. That was key for Ernie. Without a little risk, there's no reward. You know this to be true in every other area of your life. This one's no different.

## THIS IS ALL TOO COMPLICATED

I admit this is different, but it's far from complicated. Have we pushed the envelope too far, too fast? Are you feeling the way Ernie did at first? As if you're being sucked in against your will? Want to stop now? You can. Just put down this book and go back to your routine. But is that really what you want to do?

These have been challenging questions. You've been asked to consider a lot in just a few pages. If you're feeling stretched at the moment, you're in a good spot. With no pain, there's no gain. This is important stuff, worthy of the time and attention you're giving.

Hang in there. It won't necessarily get easier, but it will get a lot better. You were made for more. You are on your way.

Before moving on, let's review some of the questions we've been considering.

1. Do you ever find yourself wishing you could linger a bit longer to talk to friends about things beyond the usual topics? More personal? Even spiritual?

2. If you were asked to describe the real depth of your relationship with your wife, what would that be?

3. What if you could read other people's thoughts and impressions about you? Would you be surprised? Pleased? Mortified? Embarrassed? Would it drive you to self-examination and change?

4. Does your image of men you admire include those who cry and open up to others?

5. What might compel you to go looking for some "missing part" in your life?

6. What is your idea of a "normal" amount of faith?

7. Are you uncomfortable around those you consider too evangelical? Why?

8. Have you ever taken or considered taking a "leap of faith"? What would that be?

9. Have you considered or tried different venues for exploring your faith?

10. Did this chapter make you a little uncomfortable? Why?

# NOTES

1. *City Slickers*, directed by Ron Underwood (Los Angeles: Columbia, 1991).

2. *Annie Hall*, directed by Woody Allen (Los Angeles: United Artists, 1977).

3. *What Women Want*, directed by Nancy Meyers (Hollywood: Paramount, 2000).

4. *The Godfather*, directed by Francis Ford Coppola (Hollywood: Paramount, 1972).

5. Charles R. Swindoll, *Great Days with the Great Lives* (Nashville: Thomas Nelson, 2005), 27.

# WHAT LIES WITHIN?

Embarking on the New Man Journey requires
going "inward" and replacing what's there
with an entirely new operating system.

I admit it. Like you, perhaps, my orientation is outward. I'm not
good with "quiet time," have the attention span of a gnat when it
comes to prayer, and generally find myself looking for someone to
talk to or something to watch or read to remain occupied.

That's right, I need to be occupied. Most of this book has
been written in public places like hotel lobbies, restaurants, the
beach—anywhere I could be anonymous and unobtrusive but still
stimulated by the sights, sounds, smells, and general activity around

me. Strangely enough, my brain and creativity work best with lots of external stimuli. So, being wired this way, the self-examination "thing" doesn't come easily. Fortunately, I'm married to the best nonprofessional psychologist on the planet, which, because she's someone *outside* to talk with about what's going on *inside*, gives me an edge. Otherwise, I might have become one of those old guys you see walking down the street having conversations aloud with himself.

What comes naturally isn't always the best prescription for growth. I don't like exercise. Forty-five minutes on a treadmill seems like two hours, and all the crunching, lifting, pushing, and pulling on the other machines isn't much better. The part I like best is spraying and wiping down the equipment for the next victim, because I know I'm out of there. I know I need this, however, to remain physically fit, and I see the results of slacking off. So when I can no longer stand seeing the blob in the mirror (versus the lean machine of my youth or the gray-haired guy diving off the board in the Lipitor commercial), I finally make the long, painful trek to the exercise room in our finished basement. I do what I dislike to get what I like and need.

You see where I'm going with this. The New Man Journey is an internal rigor. The road we need to travel isn't covered by asphalt, stone, pavement, or even dirt. We can't key it into our GPS or be routed there by a pleasant computer voice. Nope, this road is discovered, entered, and navigated with a completely different set of markers, signals, and traffic rules.

## JESUS AND NICODEMUS—A DIFFERENT PARADIGM

For this new journey, let's consider the conversation that a member of the Jewish ruling council had one evening with a man who claimed to represent God. The visitor, a Pharisee named Nicodemus, arrives after dark so his colleagues won't see him. He's afraid of what they'll think. But Nicodemus has questions, and he suspects this teacher named Jesus has the answers.

We can imagine the scene. The two men settle on a mossy area under a large olive tree. It's a chilly night. Jesus piles up some small branches, surrounds them with rocks, rubs a couple of sticks together to get a fire going, and reclines against the tree. A tiny brook purls nearby. Nicodemus is surprised to realize he's nervous, but he plunges in:

"Rabbi, we know that you are a teacher who has come from God. For no one could perform the signs you are doing if God were not with him."

Jesus replies, "Very truly I tell you, no one can see the kingdom of God unless they are born again."

"How can someone be born when they are old?" Nicodemus asks. "Surely they cannot enter a second time into their mother's womb to be born!"

Jesus answers, "Very truly I tell you, no one can enter the kingdom of God unless they are born of water and the Spirit. Flesh gives birth to flesh, but the Spirit gives birth to spirit. You should not be surprised at my saying, 'You must be born again.' The wind blows wherever it pleases.

You hear its sound, but you cannot tell where it comes from or where it is going. So it is with everyone born of the Spirit."

"How can this be?" Nicodemus asks.

"You are Israel's teacher," says Jesus, "and do you not understand these things? Very truly I tell you, we speak of what we know, and we testify to what we have seen, but still you people do not accept our testimony. I have spoken to you of earthly things and you do not believe; how then will you believe if I speak of heavenly things? No one has ever gone into heaven except the one who came from heaven— the Son of Man." (see John 3:2–13)

Nicodemus would, like most of us, have been familiar with the meaning of being "born of water" as referring to physical birth. He naturally responds to Jesus's cut-to-the-chase opening comment with the response, "How can a man be born when he is old? Can he enter a second time into his mother's womb and be born?" A logical question. He was unprepared, however, for Jesus's reply: "Unless you are born of water and the Spirit, you cannot enter the kingdom of God."

Nicodemus would have believed that being born a Jew and maintaining the Law would have automatically entailed entrance to the kingdom of God. So what's all this "Flesh being born of flesh" and "Spirit being born of spirit" about?

Jesus further complicates things for Nicodemus by bringing in the business about the wind blowing and not knowing where it comes from or where it goes. I can hear Nicodemus's thoughts and see his mental contortions. *This is too complicated. I've never heard anything like this. I'm confused. However, I know You come from God because of all the miracles You perform, so I can't discount this and go about my merry way. C'mon, help me out here, Jesus.*

We can deduce from the passage, using poetic license, that Jesus then kindly cuts earnest Nicodemus some slack and tells him plainly: "Forget everything you've ever known about physical birth. This is a completely different deal. Being born of water, just being here on earth and fulfilling the Law or going to church, will not get you into heaven. There's only one person who can get you to heaven, the one who came here straight from heaven. Me, the Son of Man. The one talking to you. Why? Because I am not earthborn from an earthly father like you and all others. I am heaven-conceived by My Father in heaven, the spiritual Father. I am uniquely both God and man.

"I've given you, Nicodemus, and anyone on earth who believes in and follows Me the opportunity to be reborn in his mind, his body, and his spirit—and to join Me in My heavenly kingdom. Who knows who will respond to My message. This spiritual rebirth is like the wind blowing here, there, and all around everyone. You never know where it comes from or who will feel its effects."

This blew Nicodemus's mind. It shattered all his preconceived notions about birth and introduced another kind of birth, this one a spiritual, internal birth into a different reality, the kingdom of God. This wasn't the only time Jesus pointed followers away from the external to the internal, away from appearance to reality:

> Once, on being asked by the Pharisees when the
> kingdom of God would come, Jesus replied, "The

coming of the kingdom of God is not something that can be observed, nor will people say, 'Here it is,' or 'There it is,' because the kingdom of God is in your midst." (Luke 17:20–21)

Jesus frequently used the technique of speaking in parables to help His listeners discover and understand the true meaning of this life. He pointed people to farming and the nature of seeds, to everyday activities like the making of bread, and to accidental discoveries of buried riches to help them understand His message. They were statements like these:

The kingdom of heaven is like a mustard seed, which a man took and planted in his field. Though it is the smallest of all seeds, yet when it grows, it is the largest of garden plants and becomes a tree, so that the birds come and perch in its branches.

The kingdom of heaven is like yeast that a woman took and mixed into about sixty pounds of flour until it worked all through the dough.

The kingdom of heaven is like treasure hidden in a field. When a man found it, he hid it again, and then in his joy went and sold all he had and bought that field. Again, the kingdom of heaven is like a merchant looking for fine pearls. When he found one of great value, he went away and sold everything he had and bought it. (Matt. 13:31–33, 44–46)

*Oxford Dictionaries* defines *parable* as "a simple story used to illustrate a moral or spiritual lesson, as told by Jesus in the Gospels."[1] It was Jesus's way of showing *outward* people—including guys like you and me—how to journey *inward*.

## HOW DOES AN OUTWARD GUY TAKE AN INWARD JOURNEY?

It's no accident that Christian theologians point inward for the source of spiritual understanding and growth. In the fourth century AD, Saint Gregory of Nyssa said:

[The soul] leaves all surface appearances, not only those that can be grasped by the senses but also those which the mind itself seems to see, and it keeps on going deeper until by the operation of the spirit it penetrates the invisible and incomprehensible, and it is there that it sees God. The true vision and the true knowledge of what we seek consists precisely in not seeing, in an awareness that our goal transcends all knowledge.[2]

Saint Augustine, author of the Christian classic *The City of God*, once wrote:

I entered into the innermost part of myself.... I entered and I saw with my soul's eye (such as it was) an unchangeable light shining above this eye of my soul and above my mind.... He who knows truth knows that light, and he who knows that light knows eternity. Love knows it. O eternal truth and true love and beloved eternity! ... And I often do this, I find delight in it, and whenever I can relax from my necessary duties I have recourse to this pleasure.... I experience a state of feeling which is quite unlike anything to which I am used—a kind of sweet delight which, if I could only remain permanently in that state, would be something not of this world, not of this life. But my sad weight makes me fall back again; I am swallowed up by normality.[3]

You get it. The New Man Journey is an inner one. Let's say you respect and agree with this premise, but like me, you're not a particularly inward guy. You're more comfortable with *USA Today* or the *Wall Street Journal*, ESPN, *Midway* on the AMC channel, the Steve Jobs biography, or a good murder mystery. Put those aside and just contemplate your navel and enter a state of transcendent ecstasy like Augustine? I hear your response: "I don't think so. I'll leave that to the Brothers of the Transfiguration."

Fair enough. You are what you are. Your habits are formed, and those don't include soul-searching. So what do you do? You're receptive to examining yourself for personal and spiritual growth but simply aren't built for an inward journey. I think I can help. Consider that exercise analogy. Let's take a walk downstairs and hop on the treadmill. We'll start on level one. No incline.

So here we are. You, me, and our respective inner lives. Let's begin by getting oriented to our inner life. We know from the argument just given that we need to go there. Think of this as flipping a light switch. There are no windows down here in our exercise room, so everything is dark. We can't make out anything around us. Pitch black and silent. I'll shut up and let you get oriented. Put down the book for about a minute. Close your eyes ...

Where did your mind go? Your thoughts may have initially included, "This is a little dumb. Why am I agreeing to this?" Then some blank space, resistance, and waiting out the minute. Maybe a few thoughts and images crept in, but no flashes of insight. Overall, an uneventful exercise. That's natural, because you weren't looking for anything in particular.

Now let's try again, but with a little instruction. This time, select someone close to you on whom to concentrate, and remain focused on that person. I'll do it too. Take a couple of minutes if you like ...

Who did you choose? I picked my six-year-old grandson, Jack. I saw him in his cool little karate uniform and newly acquired green belt, doing drills with the rest of his class. Then I saw him a couple of years earlier, mowing the lawn with his toy mower beside me, while I used the real one. I had to chase him away a few times when he got too close to my mower, but he stayed right there and finished his job alongside of me. Finally, I saw him working beside our son, Blake, helping to stack wood into neat piles as they were cut and split. Jack's a worker. I could have gone on to each of our six grandchildren.

We could conduct the same exercise with many of the people and places in our lives that give us fond thoughts and memories.

Conversely, we could focus on a recent fight we had or on a traumatic childhood memory. These things inhabit the kingdom of our inner lives throughout the day whether we know it or not. If we could record our thoughts and play them back, we'd get a good idea of what occupies our inner life, what we prioritize and value and what comforts, challenges, and influences us. All we did here was take control of our inner-life thoughts for a minute, rather than letting them go on autopilot.

Now let's take this exercise a step further. Prepare for a brief conversation with God. If you already do that on a regular basis, humor me. Consider one question to ask Him during the next minute. You may not be sure He exists, much less be available to take your questions. Either way, go ahead and ask, then spend the rest of your minute trying to discern an answer …

What was your question? While unlikely in such a brief span of time, did you get any formation of an answer? Can you describe it? If you're near someone close to you, someone you trust, consider telling that person now about this exercise. Ask if he or she would like to try it. You might be surprised by the answer. Sometimes, exploring the inner life with others is easier than doing it alone.

While you were asking your question of God, I asked mine: "Lord, do You want me to write this book or is this purely my own idea?" I've asked that before and have attempted to submit everything I write to His care and guidance. I can't say for sure that this is His explicit will, but I feel a whole lot better about asking and continuing than not asking Him at all. This gives me a sense of including God in my life in the little and big decisions. I ask Him to have influence over my thoughts, words, and deeds, and the formation of my character.

This internal dialogue occupies much of my inner life. When I ask God questions about everyday things, I can't honestly say I get clear answers. What I do sense is that God is listening and that He's pleased to be included and consulted. While I certainly see the cumulative evidence of God's active involvement in my life in outward manifestations, it's in this inner realm that I've most come to understand and appreciate Him. I believe the man I've become is better than the one I would have been had I not engaged Him in my inner life.

## SYSTEMIC CHANGE

So what am I suggesting? Spend twenty minutes a day, ten in the morning and ten in the evening, closing your eyes, entering the realm of your inner life, and having a conversation with God? While there are worse uses of twenty minutes each day, it's not quite that simple. The New Man Journey requires rewiring the house, not just installing a new light switch. We need that new operating system, not just a virus cleanup trip to the Geek Squad. We are discussing systemic change. Allow me to clarify the problem and the reason for the radical inner solution that Jesus laid out for Nicodemus and each of us.

Because we're so accustomed to operating on an external level, most of us simply replace our former practical and busy thought-life elements with similar ones after we retire. We also tend to hang on to our former career life for identity and have difficulty transitioning to intrinsic meaning and purpose unrelated to what we did or do. It's a guy thing. We've established that.

Just this morning, I overheard a conversation between an eighty-seven-year-old man and a travel agent selling a polar-bear viewing expedition in Alaska. This was at a nature-photography convention in the lobby of a hotel I frequent for writing. After establishing the cost of the trip for him and his wife (also well into her eighties, with a walker) and going over the schedule and trip accommodations, he was ready to write a deposit check until his wife put on the brakes. I could see the agent's heart sink.

The conversation shifted to all the couple's previous journeys and a detailed accounting of the various nature conservancy boards on which he'd served over the years. The agent, still hoping for a sale, feigned interest. The old-timer relived his past with gusto. "We probably know more about polar bears than your tour guides," he said, leaning forward, his voice suddenly stronger. "You guys do this for a living. We're dedicated explorers. There's a difference, you know." This was his life. His badge of honor. His identity. He had an obliging audience in the agent and an interested bystander—me.

How is it with you? How attached are you to the career, acquired abilities, accomplishments, and testimonials that brought you this far? How quickly and willingly do you jump into conversations about your current or former profession and related experiences? Are you still invested there, even though your career may be over or winding down? How much of your free time do you fill with worthwhile projects and organizations that extend your professional life and contributions to society and the community? Have you thought about any of this?

I'm not suggesting you shouldn't be proud of your past career and achievements, or that giving back and becoming a contributing senior isn't of value. What I am proposing is that these, along with recreation and travel, should be the *minor* chords in your life now that you're on the homestretch. Your major focus should be to take advantage of all the time you now have—and the time you have left—to discover something you might not have found yet. I'm talking about that new creation, that new you Jesus referred to in His conversation with Nicodemus. That can be obtained only through shedding the Old Man (no matter how used to him you are) and putting on the New Man.

Our New Man, born of the Spirit and not of the flesh, doesn't cling to this world with everything it has to offer. Nor does he find his meaning and value in worldly accomplishments. His orientation and focus is the kingdom of heaven. Jesus's kingdom. His eyes are set there, and his accomplishments are measured by the perspective of his eventual destination. A whole new paradigm.

That's systemic change. A whole new operating system. It can be ours, but only if we make the choice to take Jesus up on His offer to help us implement it. I'm guessing there were things going on inside of Nicodemus that caused him to need, seek, and accept that option. Could that be where you are?

As we return to Gary's story, we'll see that he's confronting the same option.

## IS THERE STILL HOPE?

*So why does the future feel so bleak?* The question haunts Gary. He and Audrey started out together with nothing, but that didn't seem to bother them. Before children, obligations, and financial concerns overtook them, they happily scraped together what they could to get a burger and fries at Steak 'n Shake and talk about the future together. Their little apartment above her parents' garage suited them fine. They both had good starting jobs, he with the Postal Service and she with the Board of Education. They met for lunch nearly every day, bringing brown bag lunches to the park in summer and to the lake in winter. They caught up on each other's days. Nothing was wrong because they were too happy and too much in love. They had a great life.

As light rain mixed with sleet begins to fall, Gary reflects on those days. This moment is in such stark contrast to those memories. He barely recognizes the people he and Audrey have become. They are anxious, uptight, bickering at everything and nothing, grinding out every day to get to the next. This isn't the life he signed up for or envisioned. This is a drag.

His instinct is to run. Get out of there. Find a new life, a new woman who would love and appreciate him, a simpler existence where Steak 'n Shake at six or seven is the most complicated decision of the day. Gary considers this option. *Maybe I could do it? Just grab my wallet, walk through the rain and sleet to the bus station, get a ticket to someplace far away, and start life over. Audrey and the kids would make out fine. She's industrious and could likely get an administrative job at the church. The kids are out of the house and doing well. They'd forgive me for needing a new start, maybe. Anyway, Audrey hasn't been happy with me in years. She'd be better off without me. This is beginning to make sense. I could always return if this plan fails to gel—maybe.*

Gary goes back to the house and enters the back door near their bedroom so he doesn't have to see Audrey. *I'll pack lightly, grab my wallet, and back out without her noticing.* But Audrey is there on the bed, facedown and crying. She doesn't see him standing there.

Gary needs to make a decision. Should he carefully take his wallet off the dresser and slip out unnoticed? Or should he speak to her?

As he stands there, he sees the wife of his youth. He recalls freer, happier times. He sees her laughing and holding him in the park and at the beach. He remembers tears of joy at the birth of their children. He thinks of his children and grandchild on the way. This all rips through him and mixes with longing and love for his wife.

Gary isn't a particularly self-reflective man, but he's suddenly filled with questions. *Where did I miss a turn? When did we get off the road we were on? Our life together was great. Did I screw it up? Did she? Were we both in some way to blame? Has too much damage already been done, too much of a wall been built up, to fix this?*

He wants to go to Audrey. Comfort her. Tell her he loves her and that everything will be all right. He knows how she'll react, however, if he approaches her: mistrust, hostility, anguish, and hopelessness. He's seen that before. Too hard to deal with.

Gary stands at a precipice. He understands that leaving now would not be just a trial run. It would be a permanent decision. But the price of staying would be high. What to do? Is there still a tiny bit of hope for them?

## INFLECTION POINTS

Have you ever had a "Gary moment"? Can you think back to a time when major change was not an option but a requirement? When you were faced with a decision to radically turn your life around or lose the essence of what you once loved most?

I've been at that point more times than I'd like to admit. Times when my pride and insecurity (two sides of the same coin, as I've come to see) put my marriage in a ditch and required a wrecker to drag it out. Most of these were caused by me, not my wife. Of course, in the heat of the moment, I was sure they were her fault. I viscerally recall one of these from about a year ago. It was during our fortieth anniversary trip to Italy last summer. We were in Tuscany with family, who were there to help us celebrate.

We were scheduled for lunch at a great restaurant the next day. I knew it would be an expensive one. My wife is instinctively more generous with our family than I am. Sound familiar? She innocently suggested that we pick up the check. You'd think, from my reaction, that she'd asked me to buy the family a Tuscan villa. Such a simple thing. A privilege. Easy to agree upon. Right?

*No.* I made a bad choice. I said, "We've picked up too many checks already." That seemingly innocuous comment was the "match" that lit a forest fire of pent-up frustration in my wife over years of similar objections. The bad news of that story is that it ruined an otherwise great day and left a cloud over the entire trip. The good news is that I learned a great lesson about the value of being overgenerous with our family. Just like my wife. We worked it out and are now fully aligned on that front. I believe and hope I've gotten that one right for the long haul.

Remember my admonition about the need for honesty and humility for the New Man Journey? Times like these require double doses of both from me and equal measures of forgiveness from my wife.

For Gary, days and years of one fight and disappointment after another had been muted by time and acceptance. He'd become a shell of a man with a facade of a marriage, and the clock was running down to zero. Something had to change. He was at an inflection point.

In the business world, an inflection point is a time of significant change in a situation, a turning point. We come across them in our personal lives too, and often pass them by. We've all missed opportunities for crucial discussion and commitment to a better, richer life and deeper relationships.

Why is that? Because confrontation, apologies, confessions, forgiveness, and redemption don't come easily. Pride, insecurity, and hardened hearts stand in the way like guarding lions. It's easier to walk away. "Walking" might entail door slamming, harsh words, and even shouting. Or it might involve only polite and respectful silence. A classy walk, but still, it's walking away. Either way, the long-term cost is high.

Remember our exercise room? It is in inner-life exploration where the rubber meets the road. Our inner lives are loaded with inflection-point moments, and each has a time stamp on it, similar to the "Revert Document" function on this computer. By selecting that option, I can see all previous versions of this document at each point in which it was saved. Each version has a date and time. I can choose to open previous versions and work from those or revert to the current one. This file has at least twenty versions. If I choose an old one, I can see what I was thinking and writing then, before all the subsequent additions and edits.

Isn't this a lot like our lives? A continuous series of additions and edits? The difference is that we can't claw back moments in time and have do-overs like we can with our computer files. We can't go back and change our decision to "walk," or say or do something hurtful.

But what if, in our inner life, we could revisit those moments? What would we do with them? How would we address and deal with them? What would that have to do with our current life? Can these in some way converge? Can we back up and reboot past mistakes with an inner-life "Revert Document" function?

The inner life is real and active. In many ways it's more substantive than our external lives, because it's the seat of memory, emotion, and our true nature. Inside, deep down, is where we form the thoughts and qualities that affect the people we become and the behavior we direct toward others. There we can indeed revert to past inflection points to reflect upon, address, and change as necessary. Not the type of change that will reverse those decisions, but that can redeem their long-term effect. The possibility for systemic change to our nature and relationships is real. There's great power and hope in our inner life. The New Man Journey begins inside, where the kingdom is.

We are now acclimated to the New Man Journey and well on our way. In the next chapter, we'll take a closer look at the working parts that make up our inner life. Let's first review, however, some of the questions we've been considering in this chapter.

1. Would you consider yourself primarily an inward- or outward-oriented person?

2. What does your inward life look like? What themes most occupy your thoughts?

3. Do you periodically ask specific questions of God? Do you get answers? How?

4. Do you actively involve God in your thoughts, considerations, and decisions?

5. If yes, how has that worked out for you?

6. How attached are you to your past work experiences and accomplishments?

7. To what degree does your current or past professional life secure your identity?

8. Are there moments in your life that you wish you could "claw back" and redo?

9. What would you have done differently? What difference would that have made?

# NOTES

1. *Oxford Dictionaries*, "Parable," 2012, accessed October 25, 2012, http://oxforddictionaries.com/definition/english/parable.

2. Gregory of Nyssa, *From Glory to Glory*, trans. Herbert Mursillo (New York: Charles Scribner's, 1961), 118.

3. Augustine, *The Confessions of Saint Augustine*, trans. Rex Warner (New York: New American Library, 1963), 149.

# 4

# OUR DUAL NATURE

It takes our higher nature, the New Man, to tame the
beast that is our lower nature, the Old Man.

What do you deserve for the life you've lived? Think about this for a
minute.

Maybe you'll say, "What do I *deserve*? Hmm. Let me see. Well,
I've certainly been a decent guy. Loved and sacrificed for my family.
Never cheated on my wife. Was always there for the kids when they
needed me. Stayed honest in my business dealings, certainly more
than most. Sought to do the right thing. Cared about friends. Gave
my fair share to worthwhile causes. Valued my integrity. Tried to
live out the Ten Commandments. Took care of myself physically.

Worked hard to get where I am. So, I would have to say, on balance, I deserve the blessings I have. I've earned them. They weren't handed to me on a silver platter like some I know. *Yes*, I have more credits than debits to my account."

Have I captured your thoughts? This is our default, self-justified position. We're the good guys. The decent, upstanding white hats. Consider, however, the following Scripture:

> For God so loved the world that he gave his one and
> only Son, that whoever believes in him shall not
> perish but have eternal life. (John 3:16)

Many of us are familiar with this verse. It's probably the most well-known and frequently quoted in the Bible. It's flashed on handmade posters at major sporting events throughout the year. It appeared on (then) Florida Gator Tim Tebow's eye black at college football's 2009 national title game. That bold move inspired 92 million Google searches of the verse and garnered praise and scorn for Tebow. For many, however, John 3:16 might as well have read, "Have a nice day."

But reread the verse. Think about it. It's straightforward. God loved us and didn't want us to perish. So He gave us His one and only Son so we could have eternal life. Because we deserved it? Look closer. Jesus was God's only Son. His one and only. Why were we important enough for God to put His Son through all that grief and suffering? Was that really necessary? Couldn't there have been another, easier solution? What was so wrong with you and me?

Scripture says, "He was pierced for our transgressions, he was crushed for our iniquities; the punishment that brought us peace was on him, and by his wounds we are healed" (Isa. 53:5).

So much for being good and decent guys. The truth is, you and I are filled with "transgressions" and "iniquities." There's a penalty for all of that, and He paid that penalty as our substitute. "He came to pay a debt he didn't owe because we owed a debt we couldn't pay," said a wise anonymous.

Whatever else you may think about God and Christ and heaven, the love that God has for us, His lost and wayward children, is infinitely more than we could ever have for our own children. If you've suffered the loss of a child, you can just begin to understand the unfathomable love of God for Jesus.

"Here's My one and only Son," says God. "He was with Me from the beginning of time, and through Him I have created all things. He is My first and last. To Him and Him alone I have given all rule, authority, and power in the heavenly realms. I've placed all things under His feet and appointed Him to be head over everything. The fullness of Him fills everything in every way. Now I'm sending Him into the world to suffer the judgment of punishment that My creation deserves for its wretched, disobedient, prideful, and self-loving ways. Without My Son's substitution, there is no hope for any of them. Not even one. It grieves My heart to place My righteous judgment against the world upon My Son, but My sons and daughters on earth have fallen far away from Me. I have chosen this way, this drastic and extreme way, to reconcile Myself to My lost creation."

If you think I've overdramatized God's internal dialogue, consider the following Scriptures:

What shall we conclude then? Do we have any advantage? Not at all! For we have already made the charge that Jews and Gentiles alike are all under the power of sin. As it is written:

"There is no one righteous, not even one;
　　there is no one who understands;
　　there is no one who seeks God.
All have turned away,
　　they have together become worthless;
there is no one who does good,
　　not even one.
Their throats are open graves;
　　their tongues practice deceit.
The poison of vipers is on their lips.
　　Their mouths are full of cursing and
　　　　bitterness.
Their feet are swift to shed blood;
　　ruin and misery mark their ways,
and the way of peace they do not know.
　　There is no fear of God before their eyes."
　　　　(Rom. 3:9–18)

For all have sinned and fall short of the glory of God, and all are justified freely by his grace through the redemption that came by Christ Jesus.... For the wages of sin is death, but the gift of God is eternal life in Christ Jesus our Lord. (Rom. 3:23–24; 6:23)

"He himself bore our sins" in his body on the cross, so that we might die to sins and live for righteousness; "by his wounds you have been healed." ... For Christ also suffered once for sins, the righteous for the unrighteous, to bring you to God. He was put to death in the body but made alive in the Spirit. (1 Pet. 2:24; 3:18)

Let's return to our question: *What do I deserve for the life I've lived? If I juxtapose my life with that of the worst-of-the-worst human beings, do I still deserve the judgment for which Christ served as my substitute? Did He only do that for really "big" sin people, or were all my not-so-bad "little" sins up there on the cross on Jesus's body along with all those bad people's really "big" ones?*

Look at what the Bible describes as sins:

They have become filled with every kind of wickedness, evil, greed and depravity. They are full of envy, murder, strife, deceit and malice. They are gossips, slanderers, God-haters, insolent, arrogant and boastful; they invent ways of doing evil; they disobey their parents; they have no understanding, no fidelity, no love, no mercy. Although they know God's righteous decree that those who do such things deserve death, they not only continue to do these very things but also approve of those who practice them. (Rom. 1:29–32)

In this passage, greed, envy, boasting, gossip, and the like are mixed with murder, evil, wickedness, depravity, and God-hating, as though there's no difference. *Are all my "little" sins lumped in there willy-nilly with others' "big" sins? What's all that about? Isn't there a proper pecking order of sin in God's judicial system?*

If there were, would we be with the greedy, arrogant, and deceitful or with the evil, depraved, and heartless? Maybe some other, less onerous category? Are we better off if we only qualify for the first half of the list? What if a "sin barometer" measured our hearts? Even worse, what if the results were projected onto a fifty-five-inch TV screen at Best Buy? Thankfully, we are usually spared public displays of our sinful natures. Mercifully, if we have accepted Christ's substitutional, redemptive act, God doesn't continually search out and scan the dark places in our souls. Instead, He sees our advocate, Jesus, cleansing us of all unrighteousness and reconciling us to Himself: "As far as the east is from the west, so far has he removed our transgressions from us" (Ps. 103:12).

However—and this is important—God requires us to be honest with ourselves and with Him about who we really are in our heart of hearts and to be deeply cognizant of and thankful for the punishment His Son endured for us. The punishment we deserved, but He took. Pretending we don't need it and rationalizing our relative goodness is the height of arrogance, pride, and ignorance. God cannot and will not endure that.

This merits serious reflection. Reread the Romans 3:9–18 passage. It's not referring only to wife beaters, child molesters, kidnappers, drug dealers, and the like. When the Bible refers to "they," it means "us." *You and me.* Without internalizing that fact, there is little hope for a substantive New Man Journey. Self-justification won't cut it. There is only one who is justified, through and by whom we are justified. That's Jesus Christ.

To help put this in perspective, consider what Paul (writer of a third of the New Testament and considered by many to be the greatest of the apostles) said of himself:

> I thank Christ Jesus our Lord, who has given me strength, that he considered me trustworthy, appointing me to his service. Even though I was once a blasphemer and a persecutor and a violent man, I was shown mercy because I acted in ignorance and unbelief. The grace of our Lord was poured out on me abundantly, along with the faith and love that are in Christ Jesus. Here is a trustworthy saying that deserves full acceptance: Christ Jesus came into the world to save sinners—of whom I am the worst. But for that very reason I was shown mercy so that in me, the worst of sinners, Christ Jesus might display his immense patience as an example for those who would believe in him and receive eternal life. (1 Tim. 1:12–16)

How do you suppose Paul would have answered the question, "What do you deserve, Paul?" If, like for him, the pain of the reality of what you deserve is convicting you, you're doing well and on the path. The closer we look into the eye of our lower nature within us, the more we'll be motivated toward and appreciative of the process to New Man transformation.

Let's take a break before we go on. We'll be cranking this conversation up a notch when we return.

## THE DRAGON'S CAVE

Welcome back. I'm glad you returned. The New Man Journey is narrow and tricky in places. You may have been tempted to jump off and travel a broader road, one less constricting. But you've stayed and are now at the entrance to the Dragon's Cave. This is the place where we'll look into the eye of the problem—that lower nature described above.

We've established the fact that we all have a dark side, a lower nature. So, let's examine how far that evil twin has managed to insinuate himself into our minds, hearts, and behavior. Just how much are we influenced on a day-to-day basis by our unhealthy, lower nature versus our healthy, higher nature? How do we minimize the bad and optimize the good?

Most of us have already thought about and work on this in many ways. But to get us on the same page, let's define the domain of our higher nature as love, peace, beauty, hope, strength, honesty, integrity, morality, unselfishness, generosity, courage, kindness, tenderness, compassion, intimacy, sincerity, and humility. Conversely, the domain of our lower nature is hatred, restlessness, worry, anxiety, despair, weakness, dishonesty, inconsistency, greed, lust, immorality, shame, selfishness, fear, hard-heartedness, insincerity, anger, rage, and pride. You could probably come up with a better list and argue the case of some of these, but you get the point. To show the company we're keeping, here's what Paul had to say about himself on this topic:

> I do not understand what I do. For what I want to do I do not do, but what I hate I do. And if I do what I do not want to do, I agree that the law is good. As it is, it is no longer I myself who do it, but it is sin living in me. For I know that good itself does not dwell in me, that is, in my sinful nature. For I have the desire to do what is good, but I cannot carry it out. For I do not do the good I want to do, but the evil I do not want to do—this I keep on doing. Now if I do what I do not want to do, it is no longer I who do it, but it is sin living in me that does it.
>
> So I find this law at work: Although I want to do good, evil is right there with me. For in my inner being I delight in God's law; but I see another law at work in me, waging war against the law of my mind and making me a prisoner of the law of sin at work within me. What a wretched man I am! Who will rescue me from this body that is subject to death? (Rom. 7:15–24)

When Paul wrote his letter to the Romans, he was well into his ministry. He knew and outlined perfectly the struggle between his lower and higher natures. The Dragon's Cave may be our first deliberate exploration into that dark place. Before we go in, I'll need you to sign this hold-harmless disclaimer:

*I acknowledge that I am confined to the constraints of my lower nature in varying degrees, no matter how hard I try to minimize its influence. On my own, I'll never be completely free from the persistent attempts of my lower nature to compete for real estate in my life.*

*(Your signature here)*

Seriously, we can and will become exponentially transformed as we continue on our New Man Journey. As long as we are in our physical bodies, however, we'll always be challenged by the temptations and collateral damage of our lower natures to varying degrees. Paul knew, and this is true for us, too, that the ultimate liberation from his lower nature would come only after physical death and participation in Christ's resurrection. Yet he was able to make enormous strides in overcoming the influence of his lower nature.

We can too. It's encouraging to know that even this great man of God knew he had not arrived, had not fully overcome all he was saddled with in the Old Man, but he pressed on and continued the journey. Less than a year before his death, Paul wrote to Timothy:

> For I am already being poured out like a drink offering, and the time for my departure is near. I have fought the good fight, I have finished the race, I have kept the faith. Now there is in store for me the crown of righteousness, which the Lord, the righteous Judge, will award to me on that day—and not only to me, but also to all who have longed for his appearing. (2 Tim. 4:6–8)

Paul had succeeded in rendering his lower nature nearly powerless. I can just see, at the end of his earthly days, the last ounce, that final vestige of sin, being kicked over as he leaped out of his old body into his new heavenly one. What a picture. Hands clapping. Face shining. Tears flowing. Choirs singing. And a huge welcome embrace from Jesus. Paul's hard-fought battle over his lower sin-nature was worth all the effort.

Does this image of Paul's final moments in his earthly body, his victory celebration, and his reception into heaven inspire you? Does it resemble your vision of your arrival on that side? Does the thought and expectation of that momentous event make your heart beat a little faster? I hope it does. That's a great sign. You want the right thing.

You may have already glimpsed your New Man in Christ, experienced his influence and presence in your life, looked at the world through his eyes, and enjoyed the freedom, joy, and positive effect he has on others when he's in control. You may be well along the path to the New Man being the predominant force in your life. But just as with Paul, the battle between the lower and higher natures continues as long as we are in this body. It's not a matter of *if* we will succumb to our lower nature influences, but how much and how often, and whether we are properly equipped for victory in the battle.

Simply denying the presence of your lower nature and the fact that you are indeed at war is a sure road to defeat. Just thinking positive thoughts without recognizing your innate depravity and need for the work of Christ's substitutional punishment and reconciling redemption is temporal and ultimately powerless. If you've never recognized your septic problem, the effect it's having on your life, and the need you have for flushing and cleansing, you haven't really turned the corner toward living out of your New Man. This is your wake-up call.

## WE ENTER THE CAVE

Now it's time to identify, confront, and let go of those lower nature anchors, chains, and debris that hold you down, lock you up, and block your way to the New Man you were created by God to be. Just keeping our lower nature under wraps is insufficient for the New Man transformation. What's required is significant disposal of large chunks of that lower nature. There is a cleansing process made possible by the redemptive act of Christ.

So let's enter the Dragon's Cave. We'll find and anesthetize the dragon, identify those parts of our lower nature that are most problematic, cut them out, close up, and leave. We'll have to repeat that iteration numerous times on our journey. This will become a natural part of our progress, not a dreaded task.

Okay. We're in. Our eyes are adjusting to the dim light. It's a little cold and dank. And there's our dragon. He's just what we imagine him to be—a gigantic reptile with lion's claws, the tail of a serpent, wings, and scaly skin. He also breathes fire when provoked. Right now, he's curled up and resting in the corner. He's not awake or causing problems at the moment, but he's there, and he's *large*. Let's approach slowly, with our needle drawn. We'll pick a spot right here … make the injection … a little movement … and … now he's down and out. Good. Let's get to work. Scalpels out. What will we cut? He's so big. Where to begin?

Each of us has an area or two with which we wrestle most frequently and regularly. Ones that jump up and bite us just when we think we have them under control. They could be well disguised, even from us. These are more than annoying little habits. These are large veins of irritation. They aren't physical issues (although we may have plenty of those) but character flaws that have meaningfully handicapped us over the years. I'll illustrate.

My two biggies were, and still are to a lesser extent, anger and worry. I've had to make multiple trips into the cave over the years to cut off large chunks of those two fire-breathers. I have others, too, but these are the hot anvils on which my New Man transformation has been banged out. These issues took root in my dysfunctional childhood and followed me into adulthood and into the middle of my marriage and my relationship with my children. There were plenty of nasty scenes related to both—until at the insistence of my family, about twenty years ago, I took two weeks off by myself to go into the cave, with the Lord at my side, to disable their power in my life.

Are my anger and worry completely gone after multiple surgeries? I wish they were. Both still come out periodically and unexpectedly, but their power is far less intense and their length of stay much shorter, and they are now mostly contained. My wife and I have come to recognize them for the nuisance they are and have become fairly adroit at addressing them on the spot. Each appearance and defeat renders them less powerful.

What are your dragons? What character flaws have you been managing and wish were eliminated? Can you name them? Pride?

Anger? Worry? Lust? Greed? Selfishness? Hard-heartedness? Fear? Despair? Laziness? Dishonesty? Unfaithfulness? Any of these ring a louder bell than the others? Maybe yours aren't as apparent and pronounced as my anger and worry. It may be that your lower nature attributes are so well disguised that you and others don't recognize their presence, power, and influence in your life. Some, like pride, are subtle. Think about this. Consider asking your wife or a close friend for an honest opinion. Most importantly, ask God to reveal to you those lower nature areas that displease Him and ask Him what He wants to focus on first for your New Man transformation. This is a mission-critical step in your journey. If you're still drawing a blank, consider that master of impostors—pride.

## THE MASTER OF IMPOSTORS

You may be asking, "What difference does it make how nasty my character flaws are? As long as Christ dealt with all that on the cross and has forgiven and reconciled me, why do I need to deal with it? It's over and done with. I'm thrilled that he deposited within me this New Man for me to adopt, embrace, and enjoy, who will usher me into heaven. Why is it necessary for me to look into the bowels of my unredeemed lower nature and wallow there?"

Fair enough. Your theology is close. You've accurately described what Christ did for you. It's great that you see and agree with that. There are two more important steps, however, on your journey through your lower nature to the New Man. You must acquire a broken spirit and a contrite heart: "My sacrifice, O God, is a broken spirit; a broken and contrite heart you, God, will not despise" (Ps. 51:17).

A broken spirit and a conscience-stricken heart (we'll call that humility) are the polar opposites of *pride*. Pride lives at the heart of our lower nature. Pride is the prickly essence of what keeps us from God. Pride defends us from the guilt and judgment we deserve for our lower nature preferences and submissions. Pride has a fortified, well-armed castle that defends against hatreds, persecutions, and accusations by others as well as our own self-accusations, self-hatred, and self-delusions.

If we lack *humility*, a heartfelt recognition of our hopelessness outside of Christ's redemptive act, *pride* is the necessary operating system that keeps us going. Remove our pride, and we'd collapse under the stunning realization of who we really are and what we've really done to ourselves and others. We'd be incapable of functioning. We are either judged and crucified with Christ or we fend off that frightening requirement with pride.

Pride comes in many intricate, clever, and often unrecognizable forms, but all its forms have one common attribute: self-justification. We see this all the way back in the Garden of Eden:

> Then the man and his wife heard the sound of the LORD God as he was walking in the garden in the cool of the day, and they hid from the LORD God among the trees of the garden. But the LORD God called to the man, "Where are you?"
>
> He answered, "I heard you in the garden, and I was afraid because I was naked; so I hid."

And he said, "Who told you that you were naked? Have you eaten from the tree that I commanded you not to eat from?"

The man said, "The woman you put here with me—she gave me some fruit from the tree, and I ate it."

Then the LORD God said to the woman, "What is this you have done?"

The woman said, "The serpent deceived me, and I ate." (Gen. 3:8–13)

Classic blame. "She did it." "He did it." "It's not my fault." "I didn't start it." So entered the dragon *pride*. In Eden began the multigenerational dodgeball game with God. Bobbing and weaving. Pointing and comparing.

We see this in full force with our children and grandchildren. "He started it." "No way, she started it." "I hate him." "She's a jerk." Whatever our crime, there's someone whose crime is worse. Run-of-the-mill murderers in prison hate and "take care of" child abusers. So it goes.

Are your minor infractions nothing compared to your neighbors' major ones? Do you judge your neighbors ever so subtly for the lifestyle they live? The language they use? The habits they have? Pride and judgment are two sides of the same coin. They are codependents, parasites. They feed off of each other. You can't have one without the other. Defend, judge. Judge, defend. Compare and justify. Justify and defend. That's the loop. It's in every one of us in varying degrees. Who will break the deadly grip? Is there no relief?

There is relief. The path leads through the Dragon's Cave. There, we'll come to the place where we are pliable and moldable for New Man work. We won't be like Simon, the prideful Pharisee in the passage below. We'll be like the humble, sinful woman.

When one of the Pharisees invited Jesus to have dinner with him, he went to the Pharisee's house and reclined at the table. A woman in that town who lived a sinful life learned that Jesus was eating at the Pharisee's house, so she came there with an alabaster jar of perfume. As she stood behind him at his feet weeping, she began to wet his feet with her tears. Then she wiped them with her hair, kissed them and poured perfume on them.

When the Pharisee who had invited him saw this, he said to himself, "If this man were a prophet, he would know who is touching him and what kind of woman she is—that she is a sinner."

Jesus answered him, "Simon, I have something to tell you."

"Tell me, teacher," he said.

"Two people owed money to a certain money-lender. One owed him five hundred denarii, and the other fifty. Neither of them had the money to pay him back, so he forgave the debts of both. Now which of them will love him more?"

Simon replied, "I suppose the one who had the bigger debt forgiven."

"You have judged correctly," Jesus said.

Then he turned toward the woman and said to Simon, "Do you see this woman? I came into your house. You did not give me any water for my feet, but she wet my feet with her tears and wiped them with her hair. You did not give me a kiss, but this woman, from the time I entered, has not stopped kissing my feet. You did not put oil on my head, but she has poured perfume on my feet. Therefore, I tell you, her many sins have been forgiven—as her great love has shown. But whoever has been forgiven little loves little." (Luke 7:36–47)

## POSSIBILITIES

Remember Gary, our troubled postal worker who's trying to decide between walking away and committing to a deeper relationship? He's also at the entrance to the Dragon's Cave. Let's return to his story now.

Gary stands in the bedroom, unnoticed, watching Audrey sob into her pillow, considering his stay-and-confront or leave-and-start-over decision. He knows the rest of his life hangs in the balance. He hates what they've become yet remembers what they'd been before the pressures and concerns of life killed their joy. The memory of those wonderful early years lights the small space in which he stands. It's as if someone has handed him a tiny candle. The flickering flame penetrates his shell of fear and conflict. A semblance of early dreams. Possibilities?

How did they end up in this ditch? He saw all this before while growing up. Tight finances that ignited frequent family arguments and hung like a dark cloud over his childhood home. At the time, he thought that was just the way it was with families. Then he started hanging out at friends' homes on weekends. These were happier homes. There was more laughter, more love. Dennis McGee's parents were warm and affectionate with each other. The Morgans played family games and seemed to enjoy each other's company. They welcomed Gary as a member of their family. He hated leaving these well-lit homes to go back to his own. The contrast was stark and oppressive. His own family, when he had one, would for sure resemble the McGees and the Morgans. Of that he was certain.

What happened in actuality, however, was a repeat of the same ever-present money anxieties and quarrels. These came after he and Audrey had a house and family, and the bills started mounting. Gary couldn't believe how quickly he and Audrey fell into his parents' patterns. Arguments over money at the dinner table. Abrupt ends to the evening, without a "good night." Hushed bickering in the morning before the kids were up. Cool receptions when he returned from work. His life might as well have been a videotape of what he saw as "normal" as a child growing up.

*So this is what we've come to,* he thinks. The reality of their situation hits him hard as he stands over Audrey. His mind races back to games and laughter in the Morgans' family room. To the open affections of the McGees. Lunch breaks with Audrey as young marrieds in the park in summer and at the lake in winter. So much love and hope. So few concerns. Never harsh words.

Now his heart is breaking. Tears are flowing. Does he dare trust these feelings? Might all that be recaptured? Could the prison door be opening?

Audrey must sense his presence. She turns and looks up. He catches her eyes and holds their gaze. For the first time in a long time. Something is different. Maybe. Just maybe.

## THE RIVER OF LIFE

Life snuck up on Gary and Audrey. It does for most for us. As someone once said, "Youth is wasted on the young." Do you find yourself periodically seeing yourself as a young boy? An adolescent? A young man? At what point did the "adult" in you take over? Do you, from time to time, revert to the guy you were in high school or college?

We all want and need to embrace times when we took life less seriously, when we had the luxury of being a little irresponsible or reckless and had the world by the tail. These are natural instincts and relief valves. But what exactly is it that we need relief from?

What is it we are seeking to recapture? Is retirement one big relief valve?

This directly relates to that dragon we're confronting. What's the connection? Rather than explain it in words, let's make a video together. We'll call our video *The River of Life*.

Ready? Here we are in the woods with our video cameras. Before us is a wide, slow-moving, crystalline river. Let's slowly pan up and down the river. Shoot that shoreline across the river. Got the shot? Good. The river looks deep and unobstructed from this part of the woods. We see its steady, tranquil flow.

Let's move downriver. Watch out for those low-hanging branches. We're now about a quarter mile south of where we started. Let's take our position here on the bank and start shooting. We see that the river has narrowed a bit and increased in speed. Still modest, however. As we pan south, get those rock formations on the bank and those few in the center of the river. Can you see them? Our river is shallower here.

Okay, let's relocate downriver. Oh, there's a covered bridge with openings between those side planks. Let's climb up there, to the middle of the bridge, and set our cameras looking south through one of the openings. Begin shooting. The river here is quite narrow, shallow, and turbulent. The bottom's been roiled. The water's a muddy color. Waves are splashing and crashing over all those gray rocks. The wind has kicked up. Hope it's not a bad storm. That's all right, we're safe and secure on our bridge perch. Now let's focus our cameras back on the north side of the river.

What's that way upstream? Looks like a small boat heading our way. It's getting closer. A bass boat. Two men casting toward the shoreline. But the current's too fast. Put down your camera and wave them off. Warn them about the current and the rocks on the other side of this bridge.

"Hey! Guys! Turn around. It's unsafe beyond the bridge." They don't hear us. Yell louder. "Stop! Turn back! Get to shore! Danger!"

They hear us. They're yelling, "We're fine, thanks. We know this water. Fish here all the time. Thanks anyway!"

They're wrong. They don't see what we see. Let's move closer, down on the bank, and head them off before they go too far.

"Guys. We're serious. You're mistaken. It's very fast, rough, and shallow just beyond the bridge. You'll capsize and get hurt. You could even be killed. We're serious."

Can you believe it? They're waving us off. They don't think we know what we're talking about. One of them is even laughing at our panic. What are we going to do? Maybe we have time to dive into the river and reach them before they get to the bridge. But what if we don't make it in time? What if we get caught up in the current and carried downstream, beyond the bridge, onto the rocks? If we stand here, they might perish. If we dive in after them, we might. What should we do?

This river is our life. We travel it by boat. We start in wide, clear, uncomplicated waters. As our lives progress, the vegetation on the banks gets lower and closer, life accelerates, and obstacles begin to appear. The obstacles of our lower natures. We're still doing fine, however, and navigate with relative ease. Or so we think. As we continue down the river of life, we travel into areas we believe to be safe but are actually very dangerous. We've been there before. We weren't capsized. We continue into treacherous waters without listening to the shouts of warnings of our higher natures. We continue anyway. We like the sport of it, don't consider the risk involved to be significant, have earned the right to continue. We choose to defy the odds.

If only we knew. If we could see the real danger just ahead, we'd bail out. Get on shore. Get to the safe ground from which our higher natures beckon us.

Most of us are similar to those two fishermen. We're on a pleasant outing here in retirement, enjoying the scenery, catching and enjoying life's little rewards along the way, presuming that this is the way it will be until the end. And then, who knows what?

Our lower nature acts out in many ways, often undetected. That's the unforeseen danger we're discussing. We believe we're doing fine, of no harm to ourselves or others. Then, over time, our unchecked and unaddressed lower nature entraps us in subtle and not-so-subtle ways. Before we know it, our marriages become hollow or end, we find ourselves estranged from those we once loved, our circle of genuine friendships shrinks, our bad habits turn into real handicaps, or we become obsessed with our material and physical circumstances and prospects.

Worst of all, we lose our capacity to live out meaningful lives with eternal consequences. We end up with our lower nature as master, isolated from God and everything He wants for and from us. We lose our inheritance. The dragon snags us while we're enjoying ourselves. Living for ourselves.

> There is a way that seems right to a man,
> But its end is the way of death. (Prov. 14:12 NKJV)

Failure to understand and address the truth of our lower nature is tantamount to running a boat without pilot lights on a dark night. Frivolous lives free from self-confrontation, heading straight for the rocks in this life—or in the next.

Does any of this sound familiar? A little close for comfort? Could your higher nature be shouting warnings from the riverbanks of your life? If so, it's not too late to reach safe ground. Read on.

This has been a difficult chapter. We've had to slog through Old Man soul-searching and honest self-assessment to get to this point. In the next chapter, we'll turn the corner toward the homestretch of our New Man Journey. Before going on, let's review some of the tough questions we've been considering about our dual nature:

1. How did you answer the "What do you deserve for the life you've lived" question?

2. Did your answer change after our examination of the John 3:16 verse?

3. Do you consider your sins to be little ones or big ones, minor or major?

4. Have you considered how much you are influenced by your lower nature?

5. Can you relate to Paul's "I do not understand what I do" dilemma? His victory?

6. Are you able to identify the areas in your lower nature that require removal?

7. What progress have you made, or not made, in those areas?

8. How did Gary come to the place he was in his marriage? Have you been there?

9. How would you describe where you are on the river of life? Any danger ahead?

5

# THE MISSING PART

Are you ready to activate your New Man?
It's time for the Big Download.

The force of our lower nature unexpectedly shows up in our behavior. It's always something to be reckoned with. The results, over a lifetime of intrusion and influence, are disruptive at best and devastating at worst. For most of us, our lower nature has been an insidious and constant presence, has too often had its way, and has left us with less-than-ideal marriages, family relationships, friendships, and reputations. If we're being honest, we need to admit this. If we don't admit it, our standards are simply too low.

We're at a fork in the road. The left road meanders downhill to more of the same. The right path climbs to exciting, fulfilling, and productive places and allows glimpses of life in living color. Let's regroup and move on to the next part of our journey—up that road on the right.

Our grandson Jack, the little Karate Kid I described earlier, recently completed an art exercise in his second grade class. The teacher gave out paper hearts to the kids and asked them to draw the things in their own hearts. The largest portion of Jack's heart was dedicated to action figures. There was also a smaller section for his family. Then there was a little space in the right-hand corner marked "God."

Jack brought his project home and showed it with pride to his father. Our son made all the appropriate comments, then asked about that little spot for God. Jack's answer? "Oh yeah, I almost forgot about Him." Honest response.

How about you? How many times a day do you think about God? Once? Eight? Thirty? None of the above? Do you know or can you even guess? Do you consider, include, or think about Him in routine moments or only when something really big is happening? How about when you're in the woods or seeing a fantastic sunset? In moments of stress, temptation, or trial? What portion of your art-class heart would He occupy?

You've probably heard the axiom, "There is a God-shaped vacuum in the heart of every man." The saying is often attributed to Blaise Pascal, the seventeenth-century mathematician, physicist, inventor, and Catholic philosopher. What he actually wrote is even more eloquent:

What else does this craving [in man], and this helplessness, proclaim but that there was once in man a true happiness, of which all that now remains is the empty print and trace? This he tries in vain to fill with everything around him, seeking in things that are not there the help he cannot find in those that are, though none can help, since this infinite abyss can be filled only with an infinite and immutable object, in other words with God himself.[1]

The God-shaped vacuum longs to be filled with its missing part. Ask yourself: "Am I missing that part? Have I so successfully filled the vacuum with God-substitutes that I've left little room for Him? If so, what have I stuffed in that vacuum? Is all that stuff working for me? Are all those things enough? Could God bring more satisfaction than they do? If I make more room for God, would I have to give up all these other things? Is there room in there for both? What things would need to go and what could remain? How would those that remain align with God?"

These are all good questions. We don't typically assess what occupies our hearts and competes for real estate inside of us. We've come to know what we know and love what we love. Few of us reach a point in our lives where we consciously challenge the familiar places in our hearts. Most of our hearts are probably filled with good, fond, and pleasant reflections on and about family, friends, hobbies, talents, and loved ones. God certainly doesn't want to usurp those. Our hearts also contain many neutral thoughts—the mundane details of life. And then there are the bad thoughts. We'll manage those over time. We'll ask God for help with those. Isn't that enough?

You tell me—is it enough? You've already learned from our journey thus far that it isn't. These thought processes are from the

Old Man Journey. The Old Man says, "I'm not in need of radical surgery. All I really need is incremental improvement. This old guy isn't altogether bad, and is even fairly good. He's managed to live a successful life and contribute to many people, not least of all to my wife and family. We're fine here. I may fail and sputter occasionally, but generally I'm in good shape with few regrets."

That Old Man is clever. He's a good justifier. He fights for his old life. He'd better put up a battle, because he's on the block. Under judgment. He knows deep down the jig is up. Here's what Paul had to say about this in his letter to the Philippians:

> If someone else thinks they have reasons to put confidence in the flesh, I have more: circumcised on the eighth day, of the people of Israel, of the tribe of Benjamin, a Hebrew of Hebrews; in regard to the law, a Pharisee; as for zeal, persecuting the church; as for righteousness based on the law, faultless.
>
> But whatever were gains to me I now consider loss for the sake of Christ. What is more, I consider everything a loss because of the surpassing worth of knowing Christ Jesus my Lord, for whose sake I have lost all things. I consider them garbage, that I may gain Christ and be found in him, not having a righteousness of my own that comes from the law, but that which is through faith in Christ—the righteousness that comes from God on the basis of faith. (3:4–9)

Paul intentionally took both positions in this argument. He began by defending his Old Man, the one formerly justified under the law by way of his stature as a Pharisee, a zealot for the law, and a good man. Not dissimilar to our Old Man's defense. But Paul threw all that under the bus as so much trash. He could have taken great pride in his achievements and in his public positions. He had reason to be "confident in his flesh." But after being blinded on the road to Damascus and having to be led around like a handicapped person, Paul understood how his old life was built on himself and his accomplishments, and not on God. All his hard work and all his renown were garbage in comparison to the New Man that Christ was forming inside of him. Let's let Paul explain this in his own words:

> Therefore, if anyone is in Christ, the new creation has come: The old has gone, the new is here! (2 Cor. 5:17)

> You were taught, with regard to your former way of life, to put off your old self [Old Man], which is being corrupted by its deceitful desires; to be made new in the attitude of your minds; and to put on the new self [New Man], created to be like God in true righteousness and holiness. (Eph. 4:22–24)

> I have been crucified with Christ and I no longer live, but Christ lives in me. The life I now live in the body, I live by faith in the Son of God, who loved me and gave himself for me. (Gal. 2:20)

For Paul, trading in his lower nature (Old Man), with its mixed and unreliable desires, for the higher nature (New Man), now available to him in Christ, was a no-brainer. He recognized the massive difference between the two and willingly put it all on the line. He was no longer fooled and enticed by the vanity of his former life, nor was he tempted to defend that old guy.

I love this about Paul. I'm inspired by men like him, Dietrich Bonhoeffer, and others who had much to lose in this world by following Christ. They counted the cost and made the exchange. Bonhoeffer was a world-renowned theologian in the 1930s. At the height of his success, he became convicted that a greater cause than his career might require him to give up everything. As it turned out, he was right. In 1939, Bonhoeffer decided, after much inner turmoil, that he had to leave a safe position in the United States and return to Germany. He would join others in using his influence to resist Nazism after Hitler's rise to power. Bonhoeffer believed he'd made a mistake in coming to America and that he had to struggle through the difficulties in Germany with his people.

After four years of working with the anti-Nazi underground and being implicated as part of an unsuccessful plot on Hitler's life, Bonhoeffer was hanged along with other resistance fighters in 1945. His decision cost him his life, but his witness endures.

I find myself longing to come to the place in my own life where I might approach the attitude of these men. I'll probably never get to where they were, but the goal inspires me and empowers me to keep up the pursuit.

How about you? Are you prepared to kick over the traces, to admit that whoever and whatever you were in your former

Old Man is effectively worthless compared to your New Man transformation? If you are, we can fill that God-shaped vacuum together. I can think of no better beginning than to claim as our truths Paul's prayer for his beloved Ephesian brothers:

> For this reason I kneel before the Father, from whom every family in heaven and on earth derives its name. I pray that out of his glorious riches he may strengthen [us] with power through his Spirit in [our] inner beings so that Christ may dwell in [our] hearts through faith. And I pray that [we], being rooted and established in love, may have power, together with all the Lord's holy people, to grasp how wide and long and high and deep is the love of Christ, and to know this love that surpasses knowledge—that [we] may be filled to the measure of all the fullness of God. (Eph. 3:14–19)

## TIME TO REBOOT

Reread the Ephesians passage above. Now, read it a third time. I recommend memorizing it. Engrave it on your heart, so to speak. If you want to go even further, quote it slowly to your wife or best friend and discuss its implications for your life. This is my favorite passage in the Bible. My go-to whenever I get off the New Man Journey path, which is all too often. It reminds me of what's possible—"That we may be filled to the measure of all the fullness of God"—and how I can and should be thinking and living. This points me back. Calibrates me. It's my "reboot" button.

Let's develop this computer operating system analogy. Few would deny that computers have become essential to our lives. Most of us depend on them for much, if not most, of our communications, information, entertainment, personal business, and careers. Can you imagine your life without a computer? Like it or not, for most of us they've become intricately woven into just about every aspect of our lives. Yet computers are imperfect. When they hiccup, so do we. When they freeze up, we stop because we're so dependent on them. That's just the way it is. We can rail against this, and some of us do, or we can learn to live with the assets and the liabilities of the computer generation in which we live.

I kept my last computer several years past its prime. Despite all the spyware, software updates, and bug-cleansing procedures, it grew increasingly erratic and annoyingly slow. It fought me. Rather than the friendly, useful tool it used to be, it ended up an adversary.

I finally bit the bullet and bought a new computer with an operating system much less susceptible to viruses, bugs, and unpredictable sputters and failures. You guessed it, I bought an Apple. It took a little while to adjust from my PC/Microsoft world to Apple land. I became a familiar face at the Apple store for a couple of months, lining up for appointments with the Apple geeks. However, it was a great move. My computer world is now a happy, highly productive place.

This isn't a testimonial for Apple. Chances are I'd have had a positive outcome by getting a new PC with a fresh operating system, free from all the junk my outdated one was dragging along. Any new computer would have been an improvement. But I hung on too long. I lived with the liability until it became intolerable. Why? A few thousand dollars had something to do with it. The main reason, however, was that I didn't want to face the hassles of a changeover. That would entail data transfers, downtime, and new learning. I also feared I'd lose important stuff that might not have been properly backed up. Living with the demons I knew seemed preferable to the change I knew would be better. You know where we're going.

The defect in our human operating system is a serious "bug" (our lower nature) that causes regular sputters, slowdowns, shutdowns, and periodic crashes. Wouldn't we love to have a perfect operating system—one that never fails and produces only reliable and desired outcomes? Wouldn't it be great to go into the shop, install the missing part, change the default settings to "New Man," and reboot?

Of course we'd like that. And yet we resist it. Why? Because the safety and familiarity of our flawed lives outweighs the vague and inconclusive promise of our new, improved lives. The reward doesn't seem worth the risk. So we hang on, like I did to my outdated computer. We cling until it becomes unbearable, like I did to my anger and worry issues until my wife, children, the Lord, and I declared war on them.

Do we need to hang on to our lower nature–infested lives until they become so intolerable to us or to others that we're forced to trade them in? Sadly, for many that inflection point never comes. Their hand just won't be forced. They settle for muddling along with both legs in their lower nature, or with one leg in their lower nature and the other in their higher. Split straight down the middle, dragging their smelly garbage through life, pretending it's well disguised and well managed.

That's not you and me. Our New Man Journey is about being the best we can be, about being the class acts God created us to be. We were intended to live out of our higher natures. We were created to have God as our default operating system. God says to us:

> Come to me, all you who are weary and burdened,
> and I will give you rest. Take my yoke upon you and
> learn from me, for I am gentle and humble in heart,
> and you will find rest for your souls. For my yoke is
> easy and my burden is light. (Matt. 11:28–30)

This transformation, this journey, is possible. It can be done. I've seen it in others. Family. Friends. Watched the evidence of their change unfold before my eyes as God became the driving force in their lives. I've experienced it myself. We can believe this.

## A CLEAN INSTALL

Remember Tom? He, too, stood at the door to transformation. Last time we were with him he'd just pulled into the garage of his and Brandy's Greenwich home in his new Mercedes.

*What's wrong with me?* Tom thinks.

Everything in his life appears perfect, but his inner tank has gone inexplicably dry. How can that be? All his plans have come to fruition. His is a movie-script life. He sits there trying to collect himself before going into the house; he can't face Brandy like this and alarm her. This will pass. A temporary episode. *This is crazy,* he tells himself. *Pull yourself together.*

He feels like a boat drifting in Long Island Sound without an engine or sail. He grasps for buoys—Brandy. Kids. Desk. Phone. Golf. Car. Familiar markers quickly swallowed up by the waves. He feels exposed. Out of control. *Am I having a heart attack?* He feels fine physically. *A nervous breakdown? Don't panic. Take some deep breaths. You can get through this. You're going to be fine.*

But it isn't working. He's still shaking. *What's going on here? Brandy heard me drive in. She'll come looking for me. Can't see me like this. Wouldn't understand. She'd freak out.* He closes his eyes and drifts. Out, out, out. Away from land toward the horizon. The waves are bigger, stronger. His boat rolls over them. *Where is this going? How long have I been here? How long will this last? Things like this don't happen to people like me. What should I do? God?*

Tom isn't a particularly religious man. He believes in God, considers himself a Christian, and occasionally attends a nearby Congregational church with Brandy and the kids. He doesn't think much about matters of faith beyond that. Ted and Katie were the only people he and Brandy openly discussed that type of thing with, and that didn't turn out well.

Something happened five years ago that put a strain on their relationship. Katie started attending a women's

Bible study in the home of one of their mutual friends. Six months later, Katie persuaded Ted to attend a men's retreat. Ted came back different. He told Tom he'd had a "profound experience with the Lord" and "committed his life."

After that, whenever he and Brandy got together with Ted and Katie, the conversation inevitably came around to "the Lord." What had once been an equal, free-and-easy friendship had become an opportunity for Katie and Ted to share their faith.

"Why does God always have to show up in every conversation?" Tom said to Brandy one night on the way home from dinner. It made him uncomfortable and a little angry. It made him feel as if Ted and Katie thought that he and Brandy were missing something. As if their Christianity was somehow substandard. Brandy agreed.

Tom and Brandy concluded that their lives were moving in different directions and it would be best to politely decline future dinner invitations. It would be awkward at first, but Ted and Katie would get the idea and eventually become just friendly acquaintances. He and Brandy couldn't pretend and didn't intend to change. Their friendship couldn't go back to the way it was.

Now, as Tom sits in his new car, trembling and drifting, Ted and Katie come to mind. He's always been skeptical about people he's known or heard about who've had God experiences in moments of crisis. Yet here he is, scared and sweating, considering asking God for help. He feels a little foolish. *Is this how it works? Did something like this happen to Ted?* He sees himself suspended between ocean and sky. Helpless in his anchorless, tossing boat. Eyes toward heaven. *Should I ask? What will happen? Do I have a choice?*

As Tom considers these questions, he hears, "Trust Me." The words are as clear as if they've been spoken aloud, but they come from someplace deep inside him. He knows the voice is God as sure as he knows anything. He is certain. Doubt, cynicism, and self-reliance melt away before that voice and those two words.

Tom's entire life opens in front of him. Images of everyone he loves now or has ever loved flood over him. There's Brandy, his kids, parents, brothers. Here's Ted and Katie. The waves around him become God's voice, lapping over and into his boat: "I am with you. I've always been here. Even before you were born. Trust Me. Come to Me. Invite Me into your boat. Into your life. In Me you will find hope."

"Who are You, Lord?" he finds himself saying. *Is this really me speaking with God?*

The answer comes. "I am Jesus. I have come to give you life, and to give it abundantly."

"Why me? I'm not worthy. I am … " He stumbles over the next word, but it forces itself up and out from someplace in the depths of his soul. From a place he didn't know he had. "I am—*ashamed*."

The word no sooner comes out of his mouth than a huge wave rushes over him, knocking him out of the boat and into the water. The water is warm and clean. The water, boat, sky, horizon, voice, and Lord all became one. He feels as if he's becoming consumed by it all and cleansed in the process. He knows in an instant that all his past and future offenses have been forgiven in that huge wave moment. He knows his life will never be the same. A new Tom has been born.

Then everything is still and quiet. His eyes are still closed. He doesn't want to open them. He isn't sure if he's still alive. He slowly opens them. There's his bike, hanging on the wall. Car. Dashboard. Garage. Entrance to the house. He's alive and home. Everything is the same, yet completely different. His experience of the last minute or hour has been real. He drove into his garage as one man and is about to get out of his car and go into the house a different one.

*Brandy. She's probably in the kitchen on the other side of the door.* His life with her will also be new. He doesn't know what will happen now but is sure it will be different. *Good.* He says his first prayer: *Lord, come with me into the house. Come with me everywhere in my life. Help me explain all this to Brandy.*

He's sure he hears the Lord's response: "Let's go."

# THE BIG DOWNLOAD

God stands at the door of your heart too. He's knocking and saying:

Let me in. Allow Me to download My nature into yours. Ask Me to become the engine that powers you. Your central nervous system. The blood that flows through your veins and the veins themselves. My life united to your life. Forget everything else. Leave it all behind. Behold, I'll make everything new. You'll never be the same. Your life will be hidden in Mine. Expect amazing and wonderful things to follow. The old will pass away. The new will come. My highest possible gift to you was the gift of My Son, Jesus. Accept that gift and activate your New Man. Your eyes will be opened to see and to grasp the width, length, height, and depth of My love. You will be filled to the measure of all My fullness.

Do you want this? Of course you do. Why wouldn't you? There's no better time than now to claim this reliable promise for your life. God's promise. What do you have to do? Simply ask.

God's requirements are disarmingly simple. We think it should be harder than He makes it. Just ask. God is a gentlemen. He loves and respects our free will. Just ask. Invite Him to make your heart His home. Ask Him to occupy your body, possessions, talents, business, finances, marriage, family, friendships, and all your relationships. Everything. Ask Him to transform all that you are and have been into the New Man you will become, and to take total control of that metamorphosis. It's a straightforward exchange and a phenomenal deal. The *Real Deal*. Your Old Man life, with all the good, bad, and ugly, in exchange for the New Man life He will provide. Just ask.

Now the Big Download. The terms read as follows:

This New Man operating system will give you complete access to God and fellowship with Him and His Son, Jesus.

No exceptions. By agreeing to this installation, you understand that your old operating system will be wiped clean. All your past and future sins will be forgiven. By accepting this agreement, you acknowledge that you wish to have all aspects of your life guided, led, and controlled by the Holy Spirit, the core application associated with this system. His nature is the complete embodiment of God's nature. There are no defects or flaws. God's nature will infuse and dominate your nature as the New Man operating system engages all aspects of your life. By accepting this agreement, you give over all rights and claims to your Old Man and agree to be completely replaced over time by your New Man. You further understand and agree that by installing this operating system you will, upon your physical death here, be raised to eternal life in your New Man body, one in likeness to the resurrected body of Jesus.

Have you carefully read the terms of this agreement? Would you like to install the New Man operating system? If so, check the box below and press submit:

❏ I agree to the terms of the New Man operating system, powered by the Holy Spirit.

SUBMIT

Congratulations. You've just charted the course to a new adventure that will fulfill you for the rest of your life—and beyond.

Now let's review some of the questions we've been considering about discovering and installing our "missing part."

1. How much space would God occupy in a picture of your heart?

2. Can you relate to Paul's lower- and higher-nature battle? Give some examples.

3. Would you consider yourself a candidate for incremental improvement or for radical surgery?

4. What does Paul's prayer in Ephesians 3:14–19 mean to you?

5. Can you relate to the new operating system download analogy? How?

6. Did you check the New Man operating system agreement box? If yes, why? If no, why not?

7. Perhaps you checked that box earlier in life? If so, did you fully understand the terms?

8. Tom's conversion was dramatic. Can you relate to it on any level? How?

## NOTES

1. Blaise Pascal, *Pensées*, trans. A. J. Krailsheimer (London: Penguin, 1995).

6

# CHOICES

Our New Man leads us to wise choices
and reconciled relationships.

In the last chapter, you may have made the choice to give control of
your life to the Holy Spirit. To download the New Man operating
system, as I referred to that changeover. I truly hope so. But maybe
you haven't decided yet. Maybe you're waiting to see what comes
next before you commit. The choice, of course, is yours.

Life is a continuous series of choices. Big ones are obvious. Go
to this college. Marry this woman. Break off the engagement. Take
that job. Start a business. Buy that company. Have children. Move to
this city. Have the operation. Buy that house. Make this investment.

Retire now. Retire here. These and other major decisions alter outcomes in ways hard to see at the time.

What if you'd married your high-school girlfriend? Chosen to start over in another city? Gone to a different college? Majored in something else? Stayed with your first company? Remained single? Questions. Roads not taken. The possibilities are inexhaustible. If only we'd known the thousands of outcomes available to us when we were laying out the blueprint of our lives and making our choices.

As a young man, I loved playing guitar, songwriting, and singing. I considered a career as a singer-songwriter. James Taylor was my musical role model. I met an agent who brought me to a record producer in New York in 1972. They liked some of my material but wanted me to make changes I considered trite and commercial. Their open shirts and gold chains turned me off. So I didn't follow through. I've wondered what would have happened if I'd adjusted my standards and done as they asked. Would I have become another James Taylor? Fame, fortune, and tours for the rest of my career? A more exciting life? I imagine that outcome.

Then I ask myself if I'd still be married to Sandy. Would I have had the same stable, full family life? Remained steady and growing in my relationship with the Lord? I tell myself those wouldn't have worked out as well. But am I sure of that? If I could turn the clock back forty years and follow through with the New York opportunity, would I do it? I'll never know. What I'm certain of is that I'm happy with the life I've had and where I am today. It's the outcome of all my choices. Most, I believe, were good ones.

Some choices, like the one I made in New York, are clearly life-altering. It's easy to see and track the results of such decisions over time. Most, however, are the small and almost unnoticed mental, emotional, and spiritual decisions we make moment by moment. Though we usually don't realize it, these form our character, good and bad. They make us who we are today and influence our lives and relationships in subtle but permanent ways.

Where do good choices come from? Experience plays a big part. Healthy people want more of the good and less of the bad. We learn at an early age that choosing bad behavior has consequences. That it's better to be praised and hugged than scolded and punished. Our choices influence the quality of our life and the lives of those around us.

While growing up, I saw plenty of good choices and plenty of bad. My father could be tender and pleasant to be with—until something snapped and he turned dark. We never knew when Mr. Hyde would show up and all hell would break loose. I figured that was just the way it was and navigated around his tantrums. My mother's reaction was to lock us in the basement or pack us up in the car for a quick getaway until the storm blew through and *Good Dad* returned.

My mother was the main target of his vitriol. He hated and loved her, but with an infantile love. Like a child with a temper railing against his parents, he enjoyed being the "enfant terrible." We were led to believe he was mentally ill, with a split personality. While a reasonable explanation at the time, it confused me because I also observed him at work and out in public. Mr. Hyde never showed up in those places. The safety and security of our home was his private stomping ground. There, he frequently gave in to his lower nature. He possessed the ability to behave otherwise but allowed self-centered, sinful urges to take charge. Bad choices.

It wasn't until I was married, and saw milder versions of the same patterns in my behavior toward Sandy, that I got it. I saw in myself some of the urges my father must have seen. The choices with which he was likely confronted and the lower road he took.

Fortunately, with the help of my wife, I learned to see the wisdom of a different path. She's gentle and loving in every respect and hates conflict of all sorts. She let me know in no uncertain terms, however, that disrespectful, rude, and childish behavior had no place in her life and our home. This was announced early in our third year of marriage, while we sat with my mother on our screened side porch with a spread of corned beef, swiss cheese, mustard, rye, full-sour pickles, potato salad, and mixed fruit salad—courtesy of my mother.

I'd just made up my sandwich and plate. It was on my lap. I gave thanks to God for the food, but not to my mother. Sandy prompted me to thank her, too. Simple enough, wouldn't you say? Not for me. Not back then. It made me feel like a child being scolded, rather than a husband being reminded. My Old Man pride and caveman defenses kicked in, coming out as, "I'll thank her in my time and on my terms. But *thank you* (sarcastically) for the lesson in manners."

Bad choice! As soon as the words were out of my mouth, my life flashed in front of me. I knew I'd crossed into the dangerous territory I later came to know and refer to as "Sandy's Red Line." This is a place you don't want to go. One reserved for those rare instances in which she's provoked to a point of no return. And there I was. I knew it. She knew it. My mother sensed it.

After a few seconds, which seemed like minutes, Sandy calmly got up, walked over, tipped my well-prepared plate all over me, and walked into the house.

I was speechless. My mother was dumbfounded. I'm sure she was also privately pleased, wishing she'd done the tipping.

I just sat there. Food dripping. Mustard staining. Lunch lost. Utter absurdity. Foolish behavior met by an appropriate response. I knew I had met my match.

That incident stood out as a declaration of war. It might as well have read, "WARNING: From this time forward, all nasty behavior will be met with a proper response." Like a defiant child, I crossed that line all too often in our early years and was justifiably smacked down. Sandy showed me the consequences of my bad behavior, of choosing to indulge my Old Man.

I've wised up over the years as my New Man has occupied more real estate in my life. I've discovered that living with love and harmony is sweeter than snarling from the doghouse. That enjoying a good sandwich with my wife is better than cleaning up a tossed one. This has been more than a Pavlovian response to punishment avoidance. It's been a conscious preference to live out of my New Man, to choose and continue to choose, day by day, sometimes minute by minute, my higher nature.

## WINNING THE WAR

Every day we're presented with challenges and choices that either hold us back or move us forward. Wisdom allows us to see the curveballs coming, step away from the plate, collect ourselves, and act out of our New Man. These are subtle, small choices, unnoticed by others. If our lower nature didn't constantly demand airtime, we wouldn't need to think about these things. We wouldn't have to be so vigilant. Yet the Old Man's always popping his head out, always seeking small victories over our New Man. Sometimes he wins. As our New Man in Christ takes deeper root in our lives, however, those times become minor scrimmages rather than major battles. The Old Man takes fewer prisoners than he used to. There's a battle waging within us for hegemony. Each New Man choice strengthens us and weakens the Old Man's operational power.

I recently changed our dental provider. The dentist we'd had for the past forty years was retiring. He was an individual practitioner with a comfortable, old-fashioned way of doing business. I trusted him. The new provider is part of an East Coast franchise operation. Our first visit entailed a series of X-rays to establish a baseline look at our condition. The new dentist found problems and prescribed treatments our longtime dentist hadn't.

When I got home, I saw my wife's recommendations were the same as mine, $300 over insurance reimbursement. She elected to have them do the regular cleaning the next day. "Only cleaning, no antibiotic rinsing, no fancy stuff. No extras," she said. I looked at her bill when she got home. They'd charged her for procedures she didn't request and that weren't performed. My Old Man popped out big-time. I was indignant and would right this wrong with a vengeance.

Then I saw the curveball on its way. I imagined myself aggressively confronting the business manager. I stepped away from the plate, cooled down, and decided on a different approach. I called the business manager, politely reviewed the situation, and discussed what had and hadn't been done. She apologized and said she'd check into the matter. She quickly called back to tell me I was correct and that a credit card adjustment had been applied. The triumph wasn't the returned money. The win was that the New Man handled the situation.

My Old Man impulse would have had the same financial outcome as my New Man wisdom. That old guy would have felt good about being vindicated, about giving the business manager a piece of his mind. He would have won the battle through his insistent bombast, but he would have lost the war.

And what's the war? To always, in everything, if possible, remain reconciled in love with everyone we know and meet. *Reconciliation— Relationship*. It's the heartbeat of the New Man.

## NEW MAN HEARTBEAT

Relationships can be fragile. We usually enter them without the slightest degree of reflection or forethought about any maintenance requirements. For casual relationships, those in which an investment isn't required, that's usually sufficient. But close ones, those that matter and bring fulfillment to our lives, demand investment. We usually take them for granted until something comes up that reveals their delicate nature. Then we either ignore certain critical signs or, if we're smart in this area, get down to the business of paying attention.

Negligence equals superficial or problematic relationships. Sometimes the damage of neglect is irreversible. Sometimes it's *almost* irreversible, as with Gary and Audrey. Let's check in and see how they're doing.

Audrey is lying on the bed. Gary carefully approaches her. She turns her head, puts one arm up in resistance and closes an eye, but keeps the other focused on Gary. He sees distrust, hurt, an inner cry for help. He also sees forty years of a life built together and the mutual dependence that brings. *When did this pain enter our relationship? Did I bring it all on? Could it all have been avoided? Is it too late?*

He stares harder at the wary, vulnerable look in that one eye. *No! It can't be too late. I won't leave.* He's made his decision.

Gary gets into bed with Audrey, wraps his arms around her, and holds her close. She resists at first, then yields. They both begin to cry. No words. Just tears. Gary sits up on the side of the bed and takes Audrey's hand. Her eyes soften.

He smiles. "How about a Steak 'n Shake?" he says.

Audrey laughs and nods. "I'd like that." She glances down, then back into his eyes, intense. "Are we going to be okay, Gary?"

"We're going to be fine. We lost the wheel for a while. It doesn't need to be like this. We can find our way back. We still love each other. We're still the same couple we were. We can get through this."

The sleet outside has turned to wet snow. As they pull out of the garage, the air between them in the car is different. Cleaner. Sweeter.

Steak 'n Shake is the first stop on their new life together. Gary opens the car door for Audrey like he'd done in the early days of their relationship. A small thing, yet meaningful. As they walk into the restaurant, hand in hand, the financial problems that drove them apart fade away for the night. For now, they're suspended in the freedom and freshness of renewed love. Gary wants to capture this moment. *Maybe if we can get through a whole night like this, it will lead to another. Maybe our relationship can exist outside our financial circumstances. Perhaps we can leave Steak 'n Shake as friends and allies.*

Gary and Audrey still had a long way to go, but that night they took a critically important step toward the rest of their lives. They chose each other. They considered the alternatives and opted for love. They saw through the embittered, hostile individuals they'd become to the innocent couple they had once been. And might be again. They grabbed hold of the love, hope, and promise of their relationship and concluded they were worth it. They left their foolishness behind.

With a little wisdom and attention, their trials could have strengthened their marriage, could have made it better and stronger. Instead, Gary nearly threw away the trophy of his youth. Their marriage almost ended in the junk pile. But they crawled out of the wreckage. There's hope for them because they finally took control and refused to accept conflict as their way of living. Gary got a glimpse of something better and fought for it.

Gary and Audrey came to a make-or-break point and chose renewal. Others in their situation choose to separate or settle. Settling for a marriage without intimacy, friendship, mutual respect, and common purpose is tantamount to giving up hope. You've seen this in marriages. Maybe it was your parents. Friends. Possibly your own. This is completely unnecessary in marriage and in all important relationships. The New Man Journey is a higher calling.

## BURIED TREASURE

Back in chapter two, we met a sixty-year-old couple named Ray and Birgit. Ray wasn't willing to settle for mediocrity in his marriage, but his first attempt at sharing his feelings with Birgit backfired. The little seed of prayer he planted when he knew he was in trouble, however, was heard. Good things are about to happen.

Ray is emotionally drained after his confrontation with Birgit. He decides to sleep on the family-room couch for the night and dozes off to the sound of the chirping bird clock.

He slips into a dream. He's in a pen with several sheep. They know him and approach affectionately. He holds each one. They nuzzle into him for love and protection. They are needy. Dependent. He needs them, too. They've bonded on a deep level.

Then, somehow, he learns that the sheep are to be slaughtered by their owners for food. He can't believe the owners can't see how domesticated they are. They're so full of love, almost human. He's deeply disturbed at the prospect of their death and the injustice of that. Yet there's nothing to be done. Freeing them isn't an option for the owners. It's business as usual.

Ray awakens, still seeing those loving eyes. The birds chirp six times.

Ray checks to make sure Birgit's car is in the garage. It is. He makes coffee for both of them. She's an early riser too, but he isn't sure about this morning. Dreading the next confrontation, he hopes she sleeps late. He pours a coffee and sits at the morning-room table. Light streams in from a corner window, which catches the early sun. He watches a downy woodpecker go to work on a cherry tree. Thinks about his now-fading dream.

*Those sheep. So loving. What do they mean?*

He hears movement in the bedroom. Bathroom water. *What's she going to do? She knows I'm up. Smells the coffee. Hope she goes back to sleep. Need time to think. Maybe I should leave? No. Have to hit this.*

Birgit comes out of the bedroom.

"Good morning," Ray says. "Made the coffee. Can I pour you some?" Silence. What he'd feared. "How did you sleep?"

"How do you think I slept? You end our lives together and expect me to sleep like a baby?"

Ray puts his head in his hands. Looks up. "I didn't end our lives together. Far from it. All I said was—"

"I know what you said. It's what you *meant.*"

He's relieved. At least they're talking. "Let me get your coffee. Sit down here." He pats the chair next to him with familiar affection.

"Thank you. I'd prefer to stand."

He gets her coffee. Light, with half and half. He tries breaking the ice with humor: "Here you go. Hot and fresh. Like me." She's not amused. He offers his left hand while bringing her coffee with his right, sensing a little softening. She takes it instinctively, then pulls away.

*This is good*, he thinks. *We can talk.*

Birgit sits on a kitchen counter stool. Ray stays at the table. She starts the conversation. "Okay. What *did* you mean?"

Ray hasn't had a chance to plan an escape from the hole he's dug but does his best. "First off, I wasn't suggesting leaving, separating, or anything of the kind. I love you. You know that. We've been through everything together and will continue to until one of us checks out. For better or for worse." He checks for a reaction.

"I'm listening."

"So, what I meant … what I've been thinking … is that there's something we could have together in our relationship … that we haven't yet discovered. Something really good. Better. Kind of waiting for us. Like a buried treasure worth exploring."

Birgit crosses a leg and takes a sip of coffee. "Go on."

"I'm not saying this very well, and I don't even know what the *treasure* is. I just know it's out there and would like us to find it. Together. Do you know what I'm talking about?"

Birgit gets up. Fills both their coffee cups. Sits at the table with Ray. "I'm not sure if I do. Maybe. I'm happy and fulfilled with our life together. I always have been. I've never wanted anything else, but ... I've sensed your restlessness. I've known something was up for a while but wasn't sure what. I thought it was just normal retirement adjustment. Then, after you slapped me in the face at dinner last night, I started thinking—"

Ray interrupts. "It felt like a slap in the face? I'm so sorry. I'm not good at this sort of thing. That must have been a very tough night for you. Anyway, you said you started thinking?"

"You have no idea! Yes, I started thinking about what I'd do if you were telling me you wanted a separation or divorce." Ray takes her hand. She starts to cry. "My mind went to all kinds of places. Going to live with one of the kids. Going to Norway. A sixty-year-old divorced woman who hasn't worked for nearly forty years doesn't have many prospects. Who'd want me? I've given my whole life to you and the kids."

Ray's crying now too. He gets up, leans down, and holds her. "Oh, Birgit. That will never happen. We've built a great life together. I just want it to be better. That's what I screwed up trying to say last night. I'll never leave you," he says with a smile, "unless it's in a box."

They laugh through their tears. She stands and they embrace. She continues: "I'm relieved to hear that. I can't imagine my life without you. So don't go leaving before me." They laugh again. "The thing is, when I realized how alone and helpless I'd be without you, it got me thinking ... *maybe there's something missing in my life too*. Maybe I should have been fending for myself more all these years. A career ... or something. I don't really know what. Maybe we both need to find something. Maybe our needs are somehow related. I don't know. All I know is, I'm happy now. I'm happy to be here with you. I'm glad we're together and that we had this out. This could be the start of something new."

## RECONCILIATION—RELATIONSHIP

Our New Man doesn't settle. He knows that relationships are the centerpiece of God's existence and, therefore, of his own. This is especially true in marriage. The New Man's standards are high. He expects the best. He loves greatly because he's been greatly loved by God. He seeks reconciliation with others because he has been reconciled to God. He doesn't seek to defend or preserve himself in relationships because he no longer lives for himself, but for Christ who enables him. Our New Man claims wisdom, his greatest ally and tool, as his friend:

> Choose my instruction instead of silver,
>> knowledge rather than choice gold,
> for wisdom is more precious than rubies,
>> and nothing you desire can compare with her.
>> (Prov. 8:10–11)

Our New Man needs wisdom to stay the course in relationships. Every day, with no exceptions or latitude for even minor infractions. Wisdom to make good choices, especially with our wives, our children, our parents, and all who are close to us. He needs wisdom for insight into volatile relationships. Forget who caused what, who said what, who did what. Muster up the humility to seek reconciliation. How often should we humble ourselves, forgive, and be reconciled?

> Then Peter came to Jesus and asked, "Lord, how many times shall I forgive my brother or sister who sins against me? Up to seven times?"
>
> Jesus answered, "I tell you, not seven times, but seventy-seven times." (Matt. 18:21–22)

Over and over and over. Seventy-seven times. It is the most basic and profound principle of transformation. Reconciliation—Relationship. If you remember nothing else from this book, remember this. Engrave it. Reconciliation—Relationship. These always have been and will be the most important choices in your life. Paul said it best:

> Therefore, if anyone is in Christ, the new creation has come: The old has gone, the new is here! All this is from God, who reconciled us to himself through Christ and gave us the ministry of reconciliation: that God was reconciling the world to himself in Christ, not counting people's sins against them. And he has committed to us the message of reconciliation. We are therefore Christ's ambassadors, as

though God were making his appeal through us.
We implore you on Christ's behalf: Be reconciled
to God. God made him who had no sin to be sin
for us, so that in him we might become the righteousness of God. (2 Cor. 5:17–21)

Gary got it. When he looked into his wife's eyes, he saw the
love of his youth. That softened him toward her and created a longing for reconciliation, a desire for renewal. He acted out of love.
God is always looking into our hearts, seeking intimacy and reconciliation. He desires a relationship. Reconciliation—Relationship.
This is the heartbeat of our New Man. The litmus test of his taking
control.

Gary chose reconciliation and relationship. It allowed him
and Audrey to stay together for twenty-five more years. Their last
day together was routine, but particularly sweet. After church,
they went to their regular place for breakfast. The waitress didn't
have to ask. She brought them the same shared breakfast they
always had, the pancake-and-eggs special. Audrey carefully split
everything onto the two plates, giving Gary the largest pancake
and the best egg. A waitress noticed and smiled at the tenderness
of their relationship. Their love for each other was obvious.

The two of them had come to a place where tending to their
love was a conscious, daily priority. They'd made a promise to one
another that long-ago night at Steak 'n Shake to never again allow
differences and money problems to take center stage. They asked
for mutual forgiveness and committed to a different kind of life.
They agreed to end each day with a simple question: "How did we

do today?" There was a rule attached to the question. Neither would be to blame for a bad day if they reverted to the "old relationship," as they called it. A thumbs-up or thumbs-down was the evaluation. No other discussion was required. Both became so in sync that they knew which direction their thumbs would point. There were plenty of thumbs-down days over the years, but it made no sense to review who said what and why. They figured they both had, on balance, equal violations, and they simply tore up each other's tickets. Their goal was to remain reconciled in all things.

They had learned, years earlier, that they couldn't accomplish this without the Lord's help. Friends had invited them to a "Partnering with God" retreat at their church. It concluded with an invitation to come to the altar. Gary and Audrey went up together and invited God into their lives, their marriage, and their finances. Increasingly, Gary found it easier to let go of his Old Man and embrace his New Man. After nearly losing something precious, he'd rediscovered a wife and a life to cherish.

It's Sunday evening. Gary turns in and is falling asleep. The gratitude in his heart overflows. *Lord, thank You,* he prays silently. *Thank You for Audrey. For my family. For my life.*

He reaches out and takes Audrey's hand. *So small and frail,* he thinks. She's sound asleep. *Thank You for this woman, Lord. She's been a gift.* He thinks of that night twenty-five years ago, how he'd gotten into bed, wrapped his arms around her, and held her close. He's grateful he stayed. *What if I'd left? What would have become of my life? Of hers? Our family? We would have missed all this. Might never have come to know You, God. Thank You for preserving us. For reconciling us.*

He looks around the room and smiles. *Huh. We started over my parents' garage, and here we are in an apartment over our daughter's garage. Without a place of our own, yet fully at home.*

The words are no sooner in his mind than he hears the Lord's response, clear as a bell: "You are indeed fully at home. You've done well. You've chosen love. You've chosen Me. Go to sleep now. Kiss Audrey good night. Tell her you love her. That all is well. I'll see you in the morning."

That night, at eighty-seven years of age, Gary's life on earth came to a peaceful end and a new journey began. Audrey joined him less than two years later.

# FORTY YEARS

My wife periodically asks me what our future looks like. I used to come up with creative and romantically interesting pictures. Now I find myself saying our future is more of our present. It seems all the logistical choices have been made and we're now living out those choices. I don't think Sandy likes that answer. She probably wants more imagination. More vision. Then again, she's thirty-eight in her mind and heart, and I'm sixty-five. I'm happy to be on Medicare, approaching the age of full Social Security benefits, and enjoying senior citizen discounts. None of this bothers me. Sandy laughs at my disposition and defies aging on every level. She's more vital in many ways than she's ever been. I can't keep up with her. I love that about her.

We celebrated our fortieth anniversary last summer. Our children had a surprise party for us. Our daughter invited us to her house for dinner. When we entered, we were blindfolded, kidnapped, and taken by a circuitous route to a grand restaurant that we all love and where our daughter's wedding had taken place years ago. We didn't know where we were until we were taken out of the backseat, our blindfolds were removed, and we saw our family of thirteen standing before us at the entrance to the restaurant.

"Happy anniversary!" we heard from the chorus. That's a moment stamped with tattoo ink on my mind and heart.

There was a reception in the garden, after which we were led to a private party room and a delicious meal. After dinner, we all watched a DVD prepared by our oldest son—photo after photo of our life together, starting with our marriage in London and winding through the years of births and birthdays and swimming parties and trips to Cape Ann. Sandy and I standing next to graduated children and grandchildren, and the two of us through the fads and fashions. Our son had choreographed my original songs to go with the pictures of our youth and our growing older together.

After the presentation, our children and older grandchildren shared their memories about our marriage. Poignant, tender, heartfelt. Tears of joy and much laughter. When it came to my turn, I was ready. I'd written a piece to Sandy earlier that summer while celebrating with our family in Tuscany. I hadn't shared it with her before. This was the perfect time. I read it to our family and to Sandy. I'd like to share it with you. It's called "Forty Years."

Our life together began forty years ago in London. How little we knew then. How naive, hopeful, and in love. The obstacles were enormous. Odds against us. We saw none of that. All we knew was that we had to be together. Nothing else mattered. The force of our love was greater than the statistics. That force could have withered over the years ahead. It could have become overwhelmed by the realities of life, swamped by the challenges of crafting two lives into one. We could have become a statistic.

So what happened? The attraction that brought us together still resembles the one that we share now, but it's morphed and evolved into this for me. I think of you constantly. My heart still leaps when I see you, even if we've been apart for only a few hours. I crumble inside when you get upset with me, because I so need to be right with you. My need for closeness to you on the deepest levels has forced me to change and grow in character to meet your standards and maintain your trust. Our love is the anvil on which God has pounded out the man I've become. That's just the way it's worked. It's been worth the thousand deaths this foolish man has been through to come to this place. There will be more deaths, but the odds are now well in our favor.

What God has crafted in our love is what He's all about. Grace trumping judgment. Forgiveness softening hearts. Selfishness giving way to sacrifice. Treating each other in ways that please and align us to Him. We've chosen Him. He's responded.

So here's how I see us. Standing together. A thousand times better than when we started. Weathered and strengthened by the challenges we've overcome and battles we've won, all with and under God's watchful eye and loving support. I no longer see us as two, but as three entwined with Christ at the center. I also see unwanted and undesirable shoots of weeds wrapped around us, trying to grow up and through us. These used to be thick vines, sometimes choking off the life of our love. However, today they are quickly recognized and pruned off before doing damage.

Now here's the best part. We now fully understand our purpose together. To be a blessing, safe harbor, resting place, and watering well for our family and loved ones. I believe we have come to that place. Our love is bigger than us. There is a lot at stake. The road for our work ahead has been paved by the past forty years. It's now wide, straight, and strong. All lights are green. Let's go, my love.

## WHERE WE'VE BEEN

Our journey thus far has lived up to its opening entreaties to go inward, to dive deep, to be honest, to discover and release our New Man. There is no other way to come to this point. We've examined and faced the reality of our lower nature. We've come to understand and challenge it for the substantial adversary and obstacle it is and will continue to be without systemic change. We are no longer deceived about our *inherent goodness*. We've seen that we are effectively powerless to rectify the problem of sin embedded in our lower nature, and we understand why Jesus had to come into the world to do for us what we can't do for ourselves. He took the judgment and punishment we deserved, that should have been yours and mine, and allowed Himself to be punished for us.

We've learned that Jesus not only addressed our sin problem but also established a brand-new nature for us to adopt—if we wish. A new nature anchored in us with His DNA, free of charge. We just ask and He comes in. He is incorporated into the structure of our lives. We willingly exchange our lower nature for His higher one. He begins to work inside our minds, our bodies, and our spirits. He works through us to reflect His attributes and accomplish His purposes. We now have a new operating system downloaded and installed. He's the root of our New Man existence.

Finally, we've begun to understand the nature of our New Man. We've seen that, at his core, the New Man is all about being reconciled in love to God and to those close to him. Uncorrupted relationships are the heartbeat of his existence. If married, his wife is the crown jewel of his relationships, the metaphor for the pounding out of the lower nature and the emergence of his new person in Christ. The intimacy and unique relationship in marriage are synched to the character and quality of his other relationships and of his relationship to God.

In the next chapter, we'll make a closer examination of our New Man. Put him on and walk around in him. First, let's review some of the questions we've been considering in this chapter.

1. What was the turning point in Gary and Audrey's relationship?

2. What was the key to their long-term success?

3. How, if at all, does your marriage resemble theirs? Would you want what they had?

4. Which choices, good or bad, have had the most profound effects on your life?

5. Which of those would you reverse if you could?

6. Give examples of how minor choices throughout your life had major effects.

7. How would you describe your future together to your wife? How would that go over with her?

8. Was there a time when you had to "grow up" in your relationship with your wife?

9. Would you say that you're applying wisdom in your marriage? Other relationships? How?

# 7

# THE NEW MAN DEFINED

The work of the New Man is the most meaningful
on earth. Nothing else comes close.

Let's return to Jesus's nighttime conversation with Nicodemus.
As you recall, Jesus shattered all of Nicodemus's preconceived
notions about conventional earthly birth and introduced another
kind entirely. This was an internal, spiritual birth into a different
reality—the kingdom of God. Nicodemus was taken off guard.
Confused but excited, he was all ears, receptive to learning about
this whole new paradigm of birth and life. We can imagine the
ensuing conversation.

"So what exactly does this new birth entail?" Nicodemus asks. "What does it look like? How is it accomplished? What's on the other side? How will it be different there? How will I know I've arrived? What form will it take? What will I look like? How will I change?"

"Great questions," says Jesus. "I'll explain. Let's put some more wood on the fire. This may take awhile."

"There's nothing more important than this," says Nicodemus. "Take all the time You need. I have a feeling nothing will be the same for me after You've finished."

Nicodemus feels safe in the presence of his new teacher. Transported by the deep brown almond-shaped eyes fixed on his, he knows this Jesus is like no other man. His teaching is truth itself. He is the Messiah. The one he's read about and longed for his whole life. His people have been waiting for over a thousand years. *Is this a dream?* Nicodemus pinches himself. *This is indeed the Messiah. Speaking directly to me. As if I were the only one on the planet. With all the time in the world for me. How can that be? Listen.*

Jesus begins. "Let me tell you a story. There was a wealthy man who had two sons. The younger one wanted his inheritance early so he could leave and explore the world. The father agreed.

"After going through his inheritance on wild living in a distant country, the younger had to take on a job feeding pigs. He was so hungry, he found himself wishing he could eat the pig's pods. This brought him to his senses. He decided he'd go back home, beg for his father's forgiveness, and ask for a job there.

"As the son approached the house, his father saw him coming and the condition he was in. His heart broke with compassion and he ran out to welcome him home. He also told his servants to clean him up, dress him, and prepare a feast and party to celebrate his homecoming.

"When the older son heard what was going on, he became angry and refused to attend the celebration. When the father pleaded with him to come, he protested that it was unfair for his unfaithful brother to get a party while he, always faithful, never had one.

"'My son,' the father said, 'you are always with me, and everything I have is yours. But we had to celebrate and be glad, because this brother of yours was dead and is alive again; he was lost and is found.'

"Now here's a question for you, Nicodemus," says Jesus. "What's the difference between the younger son and the older son in this parable?"

Nicodemus responds. "That's easy. The older was more satisfied with the life he had with his father, or was at least willing to stay on to help out with the family business. The younger was restless, dissatisfied, and wanted to explore the world and spend his inheritance. He was the foolish and reckless one. The older brother was wise in his loyalty and faithfulness to his father."

"Excellent," says Jesus. "Now here's another question. Which brother showed more virtue in the end?"

Nicodemus isn't expecting this question. "Virtue? Explain what you mean by virtue."

"You tell me, Nicodemus. You're a teacher. What is virtue?"

Nicodemus has to think. "I'll try, but You're a greater teacher than I am. Virtue is moral excellence. A virtuous man is a good moral being."

"Good, Nicodemus. I agree. Let's go with that definition. So, which brother was more virtuous?"

Nicodemus thinks. *Hmm. This is tough.* "Certainly the older son was a more moral man. The younger spent his inheritance in wild living. That must have involved heavy drinking, gambling, carousing with immoral types, womanizing, and, according to his brother, sleeping with prostitutes. Right?"

"Right. All that and more," Jesus agrees.

Nicodemus is relieved. He's doing okay. "Well, under those circumstances, I'd have to say the older is more virtuous. He didn't partake in any of that and kept himself clean. Definitely the older was more virtuous. Right?"

Jesus picks up a bowl of olives and pops one into His mouth. He offers the bowl to Nicodemus, who shakes his head. "Remember my question, Nicodemus. Which brother showed more virtue in the end?"

Nicodemus knows he's on the wrong track. "In the end. Let me think about that. Well, in the end, the younger brother was contrite and the older was angry about the inequity shown to him over his brother's getting the fattened-calf celebration with all the trimmings. He'd never been given that kind of celebration."

Jesus asks a third time, "Which was more virtuous in the end?"

Nicodemus is now stumped. He's thinking, *Jesus obviously isn't agreeing with my "older brother" answer, but it couldn't be the younger. Not after what he's done. The fact that he's contrite and his older brother is angry, hurt, and jealous certainly doesn't make him more virtuous.*

Jesus helps him out. "I can see that you're confused, Nicodemus. This is hard for you, isn't it? You can't imagine, can't accept, a standard of virtue that favors the younger brother's behavior in this case. I understand. You see conventional virtue through the eyes of how you've been taught to think by your father and your father's father. For you, morality is a matter of keeping the Ten Commandments, of living a clean and upright life, of keeping your nose clean. You've done all that. Done it well. You are the older brother in this parable."

Nicodemus objects. "Wait a minute. You're right that I wouldn't have been the squandering younger brother, but I would have been right there with the father in welcoming, forgiving, and celebrating the younger and his return home. I would have been like the father in that regard. I wouldn't have been angry, jealous, and proud like the older brother."

"That's a good answer, Nicodemus. You desire the right thing. You are moving toward your born-again man. Your New Man. However, you have one leg in this world and one in Mine. That's why you fumbled your answer. Our job tonight is to deliver you fully into the kingdom. My kingdom. Where I live and rule. That way, and only that way, will your eyes be open to see the virtues I love, the attributes that I am made of and give to My followers, My disciples.

"These attributes are as different from the world's standards and qualities as the east is from the west. The world can't understand them. It hates My rules because they threaten its standards. It hates the fact that I love and embrace the young man who sees his sin clearly and comes back, humbles himself, and apologizes to his father. That man is the New Man, born of the Spirit, who realizes his sin. This is in contrast to the older brother, who counts on his own works and good behavior and doesn't see who he really is in God's eyes. The young son is the new creature. He hears a new voice, My voice, and he responds to the world in a completely new way."

## TRANSITION AND TRANSFORMATION

We've been eavesdropping on this hypothetical conversation between Nicodemus and Jesus, admittedly using license in speculating about how that might have gone. We've seen that after this second birth that leads to the New Man, virtue is cast in an entirely different light. It's measured not by strict adherence to Old Testament Law but by repentance and grace. Our New Man is not proud of his righteousness. Instead, he is broken, contrite, overwhelmed by grace.

It's amazing that the lightning-rod term "born again" started with the inquiry of a Pharisee. Our own questions build on Nicodemus's questions and quest as we seek to clarify the Old Man to New Man transition and transformation. *Does our Old Man enter the kingdom of God when we're born again? What distinguishes our Old Man and New Man attributes? What is the work of our New Man? How do we remain true to our New Man purpose?* We want to know that our rebirth has taken place and that our transformation is progressing well. We must know that our New Man download was a good one.

The fact that we are even asking signifies that our transformation is underway. After all, who else would want to know? These questions come from hungry hearts earnestly seeking the highest and the best that God has to offer. They indicate a desire and willingness to reflect the Lord's attributes in our behavior, a desire to sync our natures with His in such a way as to make Him accessible and available to those we love, know, and meet. We want their encounter with us to be one with the Lord Himself, who lives within us and so saturates our lives as to pour out of us. This is our desire. Our goal. This is what we seek on our New Man Journey:

> Blessed are those who hunger and thirst for righteousness, for they will be filled.

> You are the light of the world. A town built on a hill cannot be hidden. Neither do people light a lamp and put it under a bowl. Instead they put

it on its stand, and it gives light to everyone in
the house. In the same way, let your light shine
before others, that they may see your good deeds
and glorify your Father in heaven. (Matt. 5:6,
14–16)

Let's test our understanding about being born again and our
accompanying New Man transformation by raising the ante. Instead
of Nicodemus sitting at the evening fire with Jesus, let's imagine that
you are face-to-face with Him. The wood in the fire is crackling, and
so is your mind as you form the most important questions you've
ever dared to ask. I'm not a theologian and make no claim to be an
expert on biblical scholarship, but I'm imagining the conversation
might go something like this.

## DOES MY OLD MAN ENTER YOUR KINGDOM WHEN I'M BORN AGAIN?

*"Jesus, You said that entering Your kingdom entails a second birth.
My first birth brought me into this world. I entered with the lower
nature I've been battling my whole life and will continue to con-
tend with and against until I finally shed my earthly body. Is that
correct?"*

"Yes. After your second birth, however, the power and influence of your lower nature declines over time. In your second birth,
your New Man is born into My kingdom with a higher nature. My
nature. That's the only nature capable of entering My kingdom."

*"But I'm still in my earthly body when I'm born into Your kingdom. What happens to my lower nature after that event? How can I be in two places at once?"*

"Great question. It's easier to explain with an analogy. I'll use one of a snake shedding its old, dead skin. He rubs along rough surfaces, catching the loose skin against the edges. This allows him to crawl out of his old skin, which appears like a snake-shaped tube. When you're reborn into My kingdom, you're effectively dead to your former life, your Old Man. He remains attached until you shed your earthly body, but his impact decreases until he's completely gone. Just as that snake waits to be freed of its dead skin, your New Man lives, grows, and becomes stronger, waiting and working to be freed of its dead skin, the Old Man. Your New Man and accompanying higher nature live in My kingdom. Your earthly body and accompanying lower nature cannot inherit My kingdom. That's why I say you must be born again to enter the kingdom of God. Once you're born again, you're no longer a citizen of this world, but of My kingdom. Your New Man remains housed in your earthly skin for a time, but he has a new body, a heavenly body, which will be freed when you rub up against the final and last hard surface of this life.

"Here's another analogy. Suppose you decide to build and furnish a new house. You sell your current house but rent it until your new one is complete. As your new house is being built, you begin occupying it. You spend more and more time there, until you've completely moved out of the rented house. That's the way it is with your New Man. His eyes are set on the mansion I'm building for him in My kingdom. His new, eternal home. He's no longer focused on this world and his rented dwelling, or 'tent,' as My servant Paul called his earthly body. The New Man no longer has an investment here and will eventually vacate the premises."

## WHAT DISTINGUISHES THE OLD MAN AND NEW MAN ATTRIBUTES?

*"Your kingdom attributes of love, kindness, respect, humility, generosity, self-control, and forgiveness aren't the exclusive domain of your disciples. They are higher nature qualities that are also abundant among those who haven't necessarily been born again. So what's the difference between the Old Man, with God's attributes embedded, and the New Man of the second birth?"*

"That's an accurate observation and another good question. I'll answer with another analogy, one from your time. Think of a gas boiler, which fires the hot water of a heating system. It has a pilot light that burns thanks to a small amount of gas that flows from a gas pipe through a small tube. The gas escaping from the tube is lit and burns all the time. The purpose of the pilot light is to provide the flame needed to light the gas coming out of the main burner. When a signal from the thermostat calls for heat, the furnace turns on and a valve releases gas into the burner. The little pilot light ignites the gas, which heats the water in the heating pipes. The pilot light itself is insufficient to heat the water in the pipes and warm the house, but the full force of the gas-fired burner can do that.

"On a relative basis, that's the difference between the Old Man and New Man operations. The Old Man is powered by the equivalent amount of God's attributes as that pilot light. He can't produce enough flame to heat the world around him but enough to know right from wrong and to exhibit good and decent behavior. The New Man is powered by the fire of the Holy Spirit. The equivalent of that main burner. He's capable of altering the lives of those around him by releasing God's power in sufficient volume to warm people toward Me. That is powerful heat indeed. The New Man is the means by which I accomplish My purpose of delivering men from this dying world into My eternal kingdom."

*"Okay, but why isn't greater 'heat' generated by these New Men, Your boilers, so to speak?"*

"My power is aligned to those who point to Me rather than themselves and their own works. I want to be seen and recognized, lifted up, worshipped, and magnified. I have to be the focus of the New Man's attention for him to represent who I am, what I came to do, and the gift of hope and eternal life given to those born again into My kingdom. The more the New Man dedicates himself to that, the greater the volume of 'heat' he will generate. He turns up the thermostat, calling for fire to be an effective witness, and I respond by pouring out My fiery Spirit. My Spirit is the flame that makes the New Man a more effective transmitter of My presence and messenger of My teaching. That's how it works.

"Some lose focus. Their attention spans are erratic. They become preoccupied with this world, trapped by their own desires, and they lose their power. Their 'burner' goes out and they lose their heat."

*"Your answer suggests that those who overtly witness for You are living out of their New Man, and others aren't. That seems limiting. How about those whose lives are their witness but who don't speak about*

*You? Also, what about those who point to You but don't reflect You in their lives? They say one thing and do another. What's the real evidence of the New Man? Witnessing for You or demonstrating Your higher nature qualities?"*

"The New Man does both. The fruit of the Spirit is love, joy, peace, patience, kindness, goodness, faithfulness, gentleness, and self-control. A good tree cannot bear bad fruit, and a bad tree cannot bear good fruit. These are the qualities by which the New Man lives, by which you can recognize him. He also knows that I am the source of his good fruit and is compelled to share that news. That becomes his privilege and his joy. Bearing fruit and sharing the good news of My kingdom are intertwined evidence of the New Man."

## WHAT IS THE WORK OF THE NEW MAN?

*"So, can the work of the New Man be summarized like this?*

*1. Shedding the Old Man 'skin' over time.*

*2. Being on fire, like an ignited 'boiler,' providing Your 'heat' in the world around us.*

*3. Bearing the fruit of the Spirit, as evidenced by Your attributes in our behavior.*

*4. Being a witness to the good news of Your kingdom and messenger of Your teaching about becoming born again."*

"Excellent. You'll do well to remember those four New Man markers. Shed your Old Man, call for heat, bear fruit, be My witness. They'll keep you in balance and on point for your New Man journey."

# HOW DO I REMAIN TRUE TO MY NEW MAN PURPOSE?

*"I know I can deceive myself into believing I'm doing those four things when I'm really not. Also, my act might be so good as to even delude those around me. How will I know when I've arrived, when my New Man is really in control? What are the signs? I want to be honest with myself."*

"This question is your best so far. It addresses your most difficult challenge: self-deception. Your enemy the Devil's main job is to render you ineffective or just marginally effective in your work for My kingdom. He can sideline you, delude you into believing you're in the game while you're only warming the bench. You may consider yourself a good follower because you resist temptation, treat others well, attend church, and talk about me. It's easy to slip into becoming one who's neither hot nor cold. Beguiled into a tepid state, a slave of this world, yet considering yourself living for My kingdom."

*"That's my concern. I don't want to be a benchwarmer, lukewarm. How can I avoid that deception and be certain I'm serving truly, faithfully, and fully out of my New Man?"*

"That involves two key things. The first has to do with sin. All sin is of the Devil. I came to destroy the power and penalty of sin. Sin has no place in my kingdom. You have to recognize and hate the sin within you that's associated with your Old Man. Earnestly desire and ask to put it all away. You may find there's sin in your life you don't recognize as sin and that you're holding on to it without knowing. You could also be secretly guarding and protecting sins you consider inconsequential. Small indiscretions, character flaws, habits you accept as tolerable, given all the "good" things you do. Ask the

Spirit to reveal those as well. All sin is of the Devil. Root it all out. Give it all up."

*"So, vigilantly seeking to recognize and rid myself of sin is the first key thing. What's the second?"*

"The second is related to the first and can't be accomplished without it. Be willing to ask for and undergo the discipline of the Spirit. The responsibility of being a New Man in this world is an awesome one, not to be taken lightly or halfheartedly. There's no second string in My kingdom. No intramural team. No casual pickup games. The work of the New Man is the most meaningful on earth. Nothing else comes close. You are chosen vessels for completing the work I began by the power of My Spirit in and through you. This requires you to be prepared and strengthened for the task."

> My son, do not make light of the Lord's discipline,
> and do not lose heart when he rebukes you,
> because the Lord disciplines the one he loves,
> and he chastens everyone he accepts as his son.
>
> No discipline seems pleasant at the time, but painful. Later on, however, it produces a harvest of righteousness and peace for those who have been trained by it.
> Therefore, strengthen your feeble arms and weak knees. (Heb. 12:5–6, 11–12)

*"What's meant by 'discipline'? What form does that take? What difficulties do I need to endure to be 'pruned'? What should I expect?"*

"The idea of Christian discipline is uncomfortable. You might be concerned about bad things befalling you or your family as a requirement for the strengthening of your New Man. Let's be clear. God does not send tragedies, sickness, and terrible things. Ever. He sends only good and perfect things. However, you are not immune to hardships. Your exposure to the vagaries of this world is no greater or no less than anyone else's. What God does, if you will allow Him, is to redeem, to make good out of every bad thing that happens to you. The New Man navigates hardships gracefully, and God has the victory in the midst of or at the end of them. In dire situations, the Spirit provides hope and a peace that only the New Man can understand.

"The discipline I'm referring to here is independent of this world's tribulations. It involves the Spirit's systematic exposure and handling of idols and character flaws in your life. Idols are those things that you treasure more than God and that prevent you from prioritizing and serving Him as you should. These are revealed to you, and you are required to turn them over for removal by the Spirit. Character flaws are the habits, practices, and behaviors associated with your lower nature, with the skin you're shedding. You already know most of those. These also are revealed, and you are required to give them up as well. One at a time, over time, the Spirit prunes away until your character reflects Mine, until your New Man matures.

"Give up sin. Embrace Christian discipline. If you are willing to commit to these two keys, enabled by the Spirit, you can be assured you will avoid the deceptions, the wrong turns off the main road, and the temptations to just quit the journey altogether. These two guidelines will be your friends along the way. They will keep you true to fulfilling your New Man purpose."

# DO YOU LOVE ME?

Our journey has brought us to the conclusion that when we're born again into Jesus's kingdom, we adopt His nature. We're infused with His DNA. As our New Man grows, we begin reflecting His attributes and become aligned to His purpose, inseparable from His values and priorities. We become synced to His will. The perfect operating system. New Man life living and growing inside of Old Man skin.

> So in Christ Jesus you are all children of God
> through faith, for all of you who were baptized into
> Christ have clothed yourselves with Christ. (Gal.
> 3:26–27)

No doubt about it. If born again into His kingdom, we are a whole new creation. There's no way to come to this conclusion and go on as usual. It changes everything. Realigns our entire life. Nothing else matters.

When a major corporation acquires another, all the assets of the acquired company become the sole property of the acquirer. The new owner evaluates the people, products, lines of business, and other assets it considers worthy of retention and sells or sheds the rest. That which is retained is aligned to the strategic purposes of the acquirer and incorporates the new owner's name, systems, procedures, and culture. Unless the acquired business is to remain an independent operating unit, within several years the acquired company is fully assimilated and reflects the acquirer in every respect. The former company is gone. No longer a legal entity. As if it never existed independent of the surviving entity. Some acquisition integrations go better than others, but all eventually take. The new owner sees to that.

That's how it is when we agree to be born again, to be blood-bought by Jesus and assimilated into His kingdom. We give up all rights to our former life. He retains what's useful for His purposes, aligns that to His will, and sheds the rest. He gives us His name (Christian), nature (attributes), strategic purpose (kingdom building), operating manual (Bible), and position (disciple). The integration process takes place over our lifetimes but is eventually complete. The Old Man skin is finally shed. The more cooperative we are, the better it goes. The closer we get to our new owner, the more we like the deal and take to our new position. Peter learned that lesson early on.

Peter was probably Jesus's most enthusiastic disciple. Quick to follow, early to recognize him as Messiah, jumping out of boats to get to Him, asking Him to wash his whole body and not just his feet, cutting off the ear of the high priest's servant at the time of Jesus's arrest. When push came to shove at Jesus's inquisition and his own life was at stake, however, Peter denied he even knew a man called Jesus and chose to preserve himself rather than to die along with Him. You know the backstory. On the night of His arrest, after Jesus's last supper with the Twelve, He explained to them what was about to happen:

> "My children, I will be with you only a little longer.
> You will look for me, and just as I told the Jews, so I
> tell you now: Where I am going, you cannot come.
> "A new command I give you: Love one another.
> As I have loved you, so you must love one another.

By this everyone will know that you are my disciples, if you love one another."

Simon Peter asked him, "Lord, where are you going?"

Jesus replied, "Where I am going, you cannot follow now, but you will follow later."

Peter asked, "Lord, why can't I follow you now? I will lay down my life for you."

Then Jesus answered, "Will you really lay down your life for me? Very truly I tell you, before the rooster crows, you will disown me three times!" (John 13:33–38)

Of course, Peter did end up denying being Jesus's disciple. After all the commitments, proclamations of belief, words of love, and to-the-death pronouncements, he failed to follow through when something more than outward show was on the line. Peter knew this. When it was all over, he cried bitterly. His shame must have been unbearable. He must have thought, *How could I do it? Of all of us, I'm the one who should have remained with Him in His hour of need. After all He did for me, I let Him down in the end. If only I could have the chance again. I'd have stormed the gates to rescue Him from His accusers and murderers. I'd have died trying. He would have seen and known how much I loved Him. He might still be alive. Now He's gone. It's over. Too late. Everything we were working for has failed. How can I live with myself now?*

Then the impossible happened. Can't you hear Peter's thoughts on that early Sunday morning? *Jesus is alive! Resurrected from the dead!*

*What He said has come true. All the pieces are coming together. He is Messiah after all. Now what? Everything's about to change! We are a key part of this. He's going to tell us what to do—but He'll probably cut me out. He certainly should. I would.*

Jesus appeared to His disciples on the evening of the first day of the week following His burial. They were all together at the time, behind locked doors for fear of the Jews coming to kill them. They were overjoyed to see Him. We know He spoke with them, breathed the Holy Spirit on them, and gave instructions. We can imagine Peter, guilty and self-conscious, hanging back a bit at this first appearance. Jesus must have noticed.

On an evening sometime later, six of the disciples, including Peter, were together at the Sea of Galilee. They decided to go fishing but didn't catch anything all night. Early the next morning, Jesus appeared on the shore, though they didn't know it was Him. He'd made a fire and prepared a breakfast of fish and bread for them. The fishermen were about a hundred yards from shore when Jesus told them where to throw their nets to make a large catch. John suddenly recognized Jesus and said, "It's the Lord." Peter jumped in the water and swam to shore while the others followed by boat. They all sat together and ate a seaside breakfast prepared by Jesus. Peter was about to receive a profound lesson.

Imagine the scene. The other disciples know about Peter's denial of their master. Peter's lost all credibility. Just a cut above Judas. They all sit around the fire together. Pregnant silence. Jesus takes Peter for a little walk along the shore. John follows from a distance, trying to hear their conversation. Jesus asks Peter, "Simon son of John, do you love Me more than these?"

Peter knows he's on a short leash with the Lord. He's already deeply humiliated. Now this. From the Lord himself. With John watching. If there'd been a hole deep enough to crawl into, he would have. Nowhere to run. The question is an indictment. The Lord might as well have said, "Simon son of John, if you loved Me the way you professed, you wouldn't have denied Me in My hour of need." Peter's not even certain what the Lord is referring to. *More than these?* he thinks. *These fishing nets and this large catch? My boat and livelihood? Do I love Him more than my friends here? Do I love Him more than they do? Maybe He means all that.*

Peter's head is spinning. He feels small. Musters up the only answer he can. "Yes, I love You." Knows it's weak. Hopes it's over.

He hears Jesus's response: "Feed My lambs." He's completely caught off guard. Looks toward John for help. John's eyes go down. He doesn't understand either.

Jesus asks again: "Simon son of John, do you love Me?"

The Lord grasps Peter's head in his hands. Holds it tightly. Tears come to Peter's eyes. His heart pounds. He looks up at Jesus. Eyes lock. John still watching.

"Yes, Lord," Peter says, his voice breaking. "You know that I love You."

"Take care of My sheep." The words pierce Peter's ears. Reverberate in echoes. *Take care of My sheep. Take care of My sheep.* He feels trapped. *What should I say? I don't know what to say. I'm failing this test.*

He hears it a third time: "Simon son of John, do you love Me?"

Peter feels the life flowing out of him. His body drained of blood. Nothing left. He can barely speak. Through heavy tears, he says, "Lord, You know all things. You know that I love You."

*Feed His sheep.* Hope stirs. *He referred to himself as the Good Shepherd. He wants me to feed His flock. He's entrusting His followers to me. After all I've done. He's forgiving me and giving me this responsibility.*

Peter feels the life coming back into him. New, warm blood flowing into his body. Astonishing peace. He hears something about stretching out his hands when he's old. Being dressed and led by others. *Could he be referring to my death? Could I have another chance to die for Him?* He hopes he will. Then, the sweetest words he's ever heard. Filling his heart and mind to overflowing. "Follow Me."

Reconciled. Restored.

"Yes, Lord. Anywhere. Thank You. I'm ready—now."

## TIPPING POINT

What happened to Peter in that brief, life-altering interaction with Jesus? He grew up. His moment in the sun had expired with the horrific events of Jesus's crucifixion and death. Peter had gone from leader to exile, loved to despised, admired to shamed. Then, with Jesus's resurrection, there was new hope for Israel. Only Peter would play no meaningful part. He'd blown all possibility of that. He was, in a word, broken. To the core.

Jesus saw through Peter's ghostly, guilty Old Man and addressed his New Man. The old Peter had been wrapped up in himself. His gifts were great. Faith. Insight. Charisma. Physical strength. Willpower. Passion. Leadership. Strengths on which he relied. Assets of a former life where he was at center stage. All his gifts and glories were useless in Jesus's kingdom. Only one thing mattered now. One commandment. One purpose. One requirement for following Jesus again: "Feed My sheep."

Peter understood. He walked out of his old skin, forgiven, given great responsibility. To feed, to pasture, to protect, and to teach was his work. Jesus trusted him with this. Nothing else mattered.

Jesus's "sheep" are those who hear His voice and follow Him. The shepherd analogy holds up as well today as it did then. Two thousand years have passed, but nothing has changed. Jesus is the same yesterday, today, and tomorrow. Countless numbers of His sheep have heard Him call and followed. We are among them. Here we are. What's He saying?

> What do you think? If a man owns a hundred sheep, and one of them wanders away, will he not leave the ninety-nine on the hills and go to look for the one that wandered off? And if he finds it, truly I tell you, he is happier about that one sheep than about the ninety-nine that did not wander off. In the same way your Father in heaven is not willing that any of these little ones should perish. (Matt. 18:12–14)

And how will we respond? Will we, like Peter, take Jesus's commandment seriously? Believe that He'll give us everything necessary for the job? Leave our Old Man behind? Put on our New Man—take His hand—and follow?

We've been on this journey together. Asked good questions. Gotten answers. Agreed to shed our Old Man with his lower nature. To be reborn into Jesus's kingdom as a New Man branded with His nature. To seek reconciliation in important relationships. Apply wisdom in all our key choices. Live victorious lives in Christ. Become completely aligned with His purpose. Feed His sheep.

Feed His sheep? *Wait.*

This feeding-sheep thing implies sharing the good news of Jesus's kingdom with friends, family, and even strangers. Being witnesses to the changes Christ has made in our lives since choosing to follow Him. Leading others down the narrow path to Him. Nurturing and developing new followers in their faith.

These responsibilities are different. Another level. Aren't they the duties of ministers, priests, missionaries, theologians, Bible teachers, and evangelists? Those with special callings, education, and training? Not us. We're not professionals. We'll be faithful in all other aspects of our New Man purpose. Leave sheep feeding to qualified shepherds. Men like Peter.

Men like Peter? He, Andrew, James, and John all fished for a living. Matthew was a tax collector and publican. None of the men Jesus chose to be his closest companions were successful in the world of religion, although there were plenty of those available. Jesus didn't choose men who met the requirements of the world, academia, or the religious establishment. He looked for men untrained in accepted methods, untainted by the stereotypes and prejudices of accredited thinking. Men like you and me.

Suppose Peter had responded to Jesus's admonition to take care of His sheep like this: "Lord, I'm not comfortable with that. Not qualified. Being responsible for the calling, care, and tending of Your followers isn't in my wheelhouse. I'm a simple man. Not well educated in these matters. You can do better. I'll follow You anywhere, but please don't give me this responsibility."

What would Jesus have done? What would have become of Peter? Fortunately, Peter heard and accepted. He didn't equivocate or qualify his response to Jesus's call and command. Of course, Peter and his fellow disciples went on to take the good news about Jesus of Nazareth all over the known world. From Jerusalem to Africa to India to Gaul to Rome to Londinium up across the channel, in just a generation. They followed his commandment to go, call, and feed.

They're now gone, but the work of the New Man goes on. That's where we come in. Not someone else. We're just like Peter, Andrew, James, John, Matthew, and millions of others who've been born again into Jesus's kingdom and empowered by His spirit to call and feed His sheep. Like Peter, we're now at a tipping point in our journey. A line has been drawn here. Are we willing to give up our reputations as regular guys? Regular guys don't go around witnessing about how Jesus has changed their lives. They don't enter into conversations with others about something as intimate and personal as their faith. That's sacred, private territory. The last thing we want to be considered by our friends and family is a religious fanatic.

I was in a similar spot ten years ago. I'd just semiretired and was considering the rest of my life. I'd been a Christian for over thirty years and took my faith seriously. I'd won many battles over my lower nature and was increasingly living out of my New Man nature. I was experienced in sharing my faith when presented with opportunities and had led others to Christ for years. However, there was a problem. There was a wall between my Christian "club" and my golf club. I could move easily and talk openly about my faith among fellow believers and many others, but I had to be more private and discreet with golf friends. I loved both worlds. Both sets of friends. I was conflicted. Then I heard "Follow Me," and Men's Golf Fellowship (MGF) was born.

It started with a few conversations with golf friends about the idea of conducting breakfasts and discussions in golf clubs that focused on the Lord. Several of us started MGF groups in our own clubs. I also started a weekly MGF speaker breakfast in mine. Momentum grew quickly, and my identity in my golf club changed. Subtly at first. Then completely.

Since then, I've integrated and entwined my faith into both worlds. MGF is no longer a strange idea. With over one thousand men involved weekly in our city and MGF expanding to other cities, it's become accepted and *normal* to participate. I no longer live a partitioned life, nor do many others since becoming involved with MGF. Sharing the great news about new life in Christ has become my passion. It is the most fulfilling and exciting work there is.

I'm the same as you. Wanting the rest of my life to be the best of my life. To get on fully and completely with the work of my New Man. We can do this. Along with Peter and the others. God will give us everything necessary for the job. Let's follow Him.

We've absorbed a lot in this chapter. If you're like me, you're struggling a little with how your New Man takes root, grows, and matures under all that old skin. We'll address that next. First, let's review some of the questions we've been asking here about our New Man.

1. Before this book, what assessments did you apply to the term "born again"?

2. Have those changed? How?

3. What happens to your Old Man when you're born again into Jesus's kingdom?

4. What are the differences between a good and moral man and one born again?

5. Explain the snake skin, boiler, and new house analogies for the New Man.

6. Describe the purpose of the New Man.

7. What two things help avoid self-deception and enable one to remain true to that purpose?

8. What was Jesus's ultimate test of Peter's love? How did Peter respond to that test?

9. What's the full job description of the New Man here on earth?

10. What's your comfort level with the job? How would full commitment to it change your life?

# NEW LIFE

**As our New Man takes root, God provides
the "fertilizer" we need to grow.**

Do you have a lawn? Did you used to? Maybe you're a city dweller, condo owner, or renter who's not lawn-challenged. Maybe you hire someone to keep your lawn perfect. Perhaps your mostly crabgrass yard doesn't bother you or you got out of the lawn business with your last move. If you're a weekend yard warrior like me, however, you'll definitely relate to the tribulations and rewards of achieving and maintaining a beautiful lawn.

I admit it. I'm lawn-obsessed, never completely satisfied. Just when I get it nearly perfect, usually in late May, conditions beyond my control (heat, lack of rain, grubs, tenacious weeds) alter it for the rest of the summer. It's the second law of thermodynamics—any closed system such as a universe, a body, or a lawn and garden has a growing tendency toward disorder at the price of order. So I resign myself to two months of beautiful lawn in May and October and battle the elements and entropy (decline, degeneration) from June through September.

We have three sections of yard: front, back, and lakefront. When we developed our lake waterfront we put down good soil and used rolls of sod for that section of lawn. It's only eighty by eighty feet, but it's our most important piece of lawn because of the waterfront activity of family and friends during the summer. The richer, thicker, greener, and weed-free that lawn is, the better. For five years, the sod worked well. Then it started showing signs of strain. By the end of the sixth summer, bare spots began appearing. These got larger the seventh year. Then disaster struck. By the end of the eighth summer, hardly a patch of good grass could be found and the sod could be peeled off and crumbled in your hand.

Not good. Something had to be done.

I got Jay, who takes care of our fall and spring cleanups, involved. We took out the old sod, raked the whole area thoroughly, tilled the ground, added good topsoil mixed with peat moss and fertilizer, planted high-quality seed, covered that over with an inch more of good soil, put down straw mulch, watered every day for two weeks, and watched for new green shoots. Jay assured me this would work. I didn't have as much faith.

But sure enough, after about three weeks, slow-growing but super-hearty grass started showing through the straw mulch. The new lawn was barely detectable at first, but it grew more each day.

Three months later, our sorry, dead waterfront yard had become a beautiful carpet of fresh, young green shoots. Now, two years later, that grass is so rich, thick, healthy, and green that I need to cut it twice as frequently as the other sections. It's a great source of personal satisfaction. When our family and friends play, sit, and visit on the green, I'm proud and thankful.

My lawn is a bit like the New Man growing inside of us. Like that new, beautiful waterfront lawn, barely visible at first, it takes time for him to settle in, take root, grow shoots, go deep, get stronger, and eventually take over the lawn of a life. This is the miraculous process whereby our New Man trumps our lower nature and becomes the prevailing behavioral force of our life. It's the healthy lawn taking over what was once crabgrass-filled or, as in the case of my waterfront lawn, crumbling and dying grass.

My seed required good conditions for growth. It needed Jay's straw mulch to keep it from getting blown around and burnt out by midday sun, watering in the morning and evening, and patience. Our New Man "seed" also needs the right conditions and materials for growth—proper care, feeding, and maintenance.

Achieving a perfect lawn isn't a straight-line process. Neither is our Old to New Man transformation. Crabgrass doesn't die off easily. It, like bad habits and sins, tenaciously hangs on, reappears, and fights for survival. One step backward for every two or three steps forward. Some setbacks are the consequence of maintenance neglect. Our greatest challenge, though, is the continual battle against our lower nature, our "crabgrass."

Fortunately, as we learned in chapter four, our New Man develops the experience and skills necessary to recognize and win those battles over time. We're able to mitigate the frequency and effects of these intrusions with proper New Man maintenance. Our greatest resource in this process is the green thumb of our owner/gardener, our God, who transforms and tends our New Man. The Lord plants, tends, and brings to fruition the New Man. We become His handiwork:

> For we are God's handiwork, created in Christ Jesus
> to do good works, which God prepared in advance
> for us to do. (Eph. 2:10)

## STARTER FERTILIZER

I've tried growing new grass with and without starter fertilizer. It's always better with. Fertilizer provides the seed roots with extra nutrients that can't be found in the surrounding soil. New Man "seed" needs a similar boost. The Holy Spirit guides, directs, and assists in our New Man birth, development, and effectiveness in the world. He also provides what we need to get started on and remain faithful to our journey. This aid comes in different forms to each of us, according to our unique needs. It might come as a dream or even a vision. Perhaps a conversation. Maybe a sermon or talk that seems to speak directly to us. The context and source might be unexpected.

I recently heard a pastor relate what he considered to be one of the most powerful Spirit interventions of his life. As a boy growing up in south LA, he and his brothers were told by their mother to never go into a dangerous part of the city. Of course, this just made him want to go that much more. One day as he got very close to this area, a local junkie he knew from the neighborhood came right up to him and said, "Go home. You don't want to end up like me." That incident was a direct warning from the Spirit, through a very unlikely source, and changed the direction of that boy's life.

However and whenever the Spirit comes, the result is always a potent reinforcement of our faith by way of indelible experiences. For some, these encounters are dramatic. What matters most, however, is that we get that occasional leg up, that special lift when needed. We can count on these.

A great little allegory called "Footprints in the Sand" provides a powerful illustration of how the Spirit worked through the author's dream to personalize his experience of God's involvement in his life. It has subsequently encouraged many others as well.

Last night I had a dream. I dreamed I was walking along the beach with the Lord. Across the sky flashed scenes from my life. For each scene, I noticed two sets of footprints in the sand: one belonged to me, the other to the Lord.

After the last scene of my life flashed before me, I looked back at the footprints in the sand. I noticed that at many times along the path of my life, especially at the very lowest and saddest times, there was only one set of footprints.

This really troubled me, so I asked the Lord about it. "Lord, You said once I decided to follow You, You'd walk with me all the way. But I noticed that during the saddest and most troublesome times of my life, there was only one set of footprints. I don't understand why, when I needed You the most, You would leave me."

The Lord replied, "My son, my precious child, I love you, and I would never leave you. During your times of suffering, when you could see only one set of footprints, it was then that I carried you."

Author unknown

Remember my friend Ernie? The one with the beautiful golf swing? He also had a dream that strongly influenced his commitment to the New Man journey. Here it is in his own words:

I had a dream, early in my faith journey, during the time that I first started reading the Bible. It was short and very powerful. It was the figure of Christ on a throne. Although I was not in the dream, it felt as if I were below the throne, looking up at Him. He was dressed in a white robe and surrounded by white light. These two features were, of course, familiar to me, but otherwise it was an image of Christ that I'd never seen before. He was older and sterner. His eyes were the strikingly dominant feature … so alive … burning with deep meaning … all knowing … all powerful. They did not look at me. They looked outward. You would not say that the face was a loving and forgiving face, but it was not severe or judgmental either. In a sense, it was both. The eyes were so dominant, so commanding. They demanded respect. The eyes were eyes that knew pain and sorrow, that had total understanding. There was a sense of sadness in the eyes but also unfathomable wisdom and strength.

When I recognized that it was Christ, I was awestruck and I said, "My Lord and my God." I said those words, exactly, and it was then that I woke up from the dream and was wide awake in an instant. I had the feeling that God had just spoken to me, as if saying, "Yes, I am for real," validating the faith journey that I had embarked upon. The image of Christ that appeared to me in that dream is stamped upon my consciousness forever. If I were an artist, I could recreate it, exactly, just as it appeared to me that night. I suspect that, as I continue my faith journey, I will come to understand the look in those eyes more completely.

Have you had an extraordinary experience that convinced you about God's direct involvement in your life or encouraged your faith when you were in need of confirmation of His presence? An impression on which you fall back in times of difficulty or doubt? If so, then you know what I'm talking about. If not, you will—at some point when you need it. For the sojourners who have gone before us, the New Man Journey has been loaded with these "extranatural" encounters. Millions of experiences down through history, many shared (like "Footprints"), have initiated and facilitated growth along the way. Starter fertilizer and soil enhancement for the journey.

If you've never had an unusual experience with God and you've committed to or are still on this journey, ask God. Test His existence. He wants to help you:

Which of you, if your son asks for bread, will give him a stone? Or if he asks for a fish, will give him a snake? If you, then, though you are evil, know how to give good gifts to your children, how much more will your Father in heaven give good gifts to those who ask him! (Matt. 7:9–11)

He desires to communicate with you. He wants your New Man seed to become well established, like the fourth type of seed in Jesus's parable:

A farmer went out to sow his seed. As he was scattering the seed, some fell along the path, and the birds came and ate it up. Some fell on rocky places, where it did not have much soil. It sprang up quickly, because the soil was shallow. But when the sun came up, the plants were scorched, and they withered because they had no root. Other seed fell among thorns, which grew up and choked the plants. Still other seed fell on good soil, where it produced a crop—a hundred, sixty or thirty times what was sown. (Matt. 13:3–8)

## THE SPIRIT'S HELP COMES IN DIFFERENT FORMS

We last joined Ray and Birgit in their retirement home kitchen, talking about their marriage and their future. Ray's first pass at opening up about his feelings put him in the penalty box for the rest of the night. However, taking that risk seems to have paid off. Their mutual feelings about needing something more in their marriage are out on the table. They're off to a new and honest start. Ray, always the engineer, now goes to work on exploring where to go from here.

"Birgit, remember how much we enjoyed traveling when I first retired? Why don't we do that again? We both love to travel. We're both looking for something more. Maybe we can find it out there somewhere … together!"

Birgit doesn't answer at first. "It's a thought," she says. "How much travel are we talking about?"

Ray jumps to his feet. "I don't really know. I haven't gotten that far. Are you up for exploring something crazy?"

"Maybe. How crazy do you want to get?" She puts her hand on her hip.

Ray sees the playful Birgit of their youth. *Where's this coming from?* He suggests they go out to lunch at the Pier Café to talk it over. After they're seated, Ray offers a toast. "Here's to getting crazy."

They clink water glasses and laugh as the server, a thirtyish woman with hoop earrings, arrives. She joins in the fun. "Are we celebrating something?" she asks.

"To tell you the truth"—Ray spies her name tag—"Carmen, we're celebrating the rest of our lives together."

Carmen's shoulders sink. She lets out a small sigh. "That is sooo beautiful. Well, if I may … I pray the Lord richly blesses you both for the rest of your lives."

Ray is taken aback by the blessing. He and Birgit both thank her. Birgit even takes Carmen's hand.

"Oh, it's my privilege," Carmen says. "Now, what are we having today?" Ray orders Tacos on the Bay for both of them, one of their favorites.

After Carmen leaves, Ray comments on her blessing. "That was so heartfelt," he says.

"Yes," Birgit says. "Very sweet. Maybe that's a sign of good things to come."

Ray agrees and starts to lay out the plan he's been forming. "This isn't fully baked, so bear with me. I was thinking … maybe we could get a motor home." Birgit looks at him over the top of her glasses. "I know, but hear me out. We said crazy." Birgit laughs. *Good sign.*

Ray explains his idea of traveling in a motor home for a year and then, if they both like their new lifestyle, selling their home to make the change permanent. He watches Birgit's reaction. She's surprised, but isn't dismissing the idea. *Another good sign.*

Carmen returns to the table. "Here you go. Two Bay Tacos. I brought extra guacamole, sour cream, and hot sauce. So, how are the lovebirds doing?"

Birgit answers. "Mr. Salesman here is trying to persuade me to buy a motor home and tour the US for a year." They all laugh. Ray reaches across the table and takes Birgit's hand.

"You guys are fortunate to be so excited about your lives together," Carmen says. "I don't see that too often here. Would you mind my asking … what's your secret?"

Ray looks at Birgit, then back up at Carmen. "That's a great question. If we have a secret, we haven't figured it out. Maybe we're about to."

"I'm sorry for imposing," Carmen says. "I just thought, maybe … it was God. You see, I'm a Christian and thought, well, you guys might be too."

Ray and Birgit look at each other again. "Well, we're Christian," Birgit says, "but I'm not sure if we are in the same way you are. Let's just say we're not devout."

Carmen glances across the room. Ray is sure, considering how busy the restaurant is, that she has other tables to attend to. Yet she stays. "I'm not devout either," she says. "Not in the religious sense. I just love Jesus. He changed my life a few years ago when my husband and I were considering a divorce. I had nowhere else to turn and just asked God for help one night when I didn't think I could go on. I have a mother who really loves the Lord. She prays for all her children every day. I think that worked for me."

Birgit, still holding Ray's hand, stares at Carmen. Several people at surrounding tables are watching too.

"What happened?" Birgit asks quietly.

"Nothing at first. I didn't hear any bells go off or anything. Then, the next morning, things just sort of began turning around between my husband and me. We had a long talk and agreed to change some things."

"So … you're still together?" Birgit says.

Carmen beams. She puts both hands in the air. "We are! Praise God."

"And things are good between you?" Birgit says.

"Yes, yes. Things are amazing. Our marriage is completely renewed."

"And that's because of God?"

Carmen takes a moment to form her answer. "Let me put it this way. Without the Lord, we'd be divorced. With Him, we're blessed out of our socks. Look, you guys, I hope I haven't been too forward here. I have to get to my other tables now, but I'll be back. Maybe we could get together outside of work? I'd love for you to meet my husband."

"You weren't the least bit forward," Birgit says. "To tell the truth, you were very helpful. Thank you. Now, please, don't let us keep you from your other tables."

After Carmen departs, Ray agrees with Birgit that she's a lovely young woman and that the timing of their meeting is amazing.

"There's another coincidence," Ray says. "Or maybe it's not a coincidence. Last night, after you went to bed, I was extremely upset. We both were. When you closed the bedroom door, I felt the door of our marriage closing. I got scared—and kind of turned to God."

Birgit's eyebrows go up. "You did?"

"Yes. And then I fell asleep and had the strangest dream." Ray relates his dream about being in a pen with sheep, holding them, and becoming extremely upset when he learned they were to be slaughtered.

"Then what?" Birgit asks, eyes wide.

"That was it. I woke up—but couldn't get those loving eyes of the sheep out of my head. They're still there."

Birgit sits quietly for a moment. "I'm not a dream interpreter," she says, cautiously, "but your dream seems fairly straightforward."

She pauses. Ray says nothing but leans forward. He wants to hear more.

"It's interesting that you had the dream right after turning to God and falling asleep," she says. "I know we've always been too busy for church, haven't been what people call 'religious.' But we both believe in God. Maybe He was speaking to you through the dream."

Ray is fascinated. "Could be. Go ahead."

"Well, Jesus referred to His followers as sheep and to Himself as the Good Shepherd. He gathers and protects the flock. You're bonding with the sheep and are concerned for their well-being."

Ray sees the dream dots connecting. Birgit's interpretation resonates. "I think you're on to something. Makes sense. So what does it mean?"

Birgit leans back. "You tell me. What does it mean?"

Ray takes a bite of cold taco. "What does it mean? Maybe it means I'm one of Jesus's sheep, that He's protecting me, and …" He stops, still forming his thoughts.

"Go ahead."

"And that I'm supposed to help save His other sheep from slaughter. Or from being lost. Does that make sense?"

"Does it make sense to you?"

Ray leans back in the booth. Scratches his head. "Kind of. It's just that … well, I'm not that kind of guy. You know what I mean."

"You mean … you're not religious?"

He thinks about that. "No. More like I'm just not interested. I'm an engineer. Nothing like a minister or anything. Yet … your interpretation makes perfect sense, and …" Suddenly, he thinks he might cry. Birgit takes his hand.

"What, honey?"

"Somehow, I hear Him speaking to me … even now, as we're talking about the dream. I see those loving eyes … and they're His eyes."

Carmen returns to the table. "Hey, you guys barely touched your tacos. Were they okay? You want me to heat them up for you?"

Ray looks up. "They're fine. And we're fine. We got carried away talking about God."

Carmen smiles. "You see, I knew we were meant to meet. I can sense God's presence here. Something special's going on with you guys. Listen, I don't want to interrupt anymore. By the way, lunch is on me."

"No, no," Ray says. "That's very sweet of you, but we can't let you do that."

"Okay," Carmen says, "I'll tell you what. You let me buy you lunch today, and the two of you can buy my husband and me lunch next week. I'm off on Monday and my husband can break away from work. Deal?"

Ray and Birgit look at each other. Birgit responds. "Deal. When and where?"

Ray and Birgit don't know it yet, but the Spirit has prompted Carmen to continue to answer Ray's modest prayer for help—a process that began with his dream. Carmen is the right person, at the right time, for the job.

## STARTING FROM SCRATCH

My friend Michael Cardone Jr. owns the largest automotive parts remanufacturing company in the world. Cardone Industries specializes in taking thousands of used parts (brakes, drivetrains, electronics, fuel and air systems, motors, pumps, steering systems), making them like new, and distributing them through automotive parts retail chains. This entails disassembling, cleaning, repairing, inspecting, reassembling, and testing the old part. Weaknesses and flaws are discovered and improved. The result is as good as or better than the original, at 30 to 50 percent less cost.

As attractive as this proposition is in the automotive parts world, no such option exists in the New Man environment we're considering. Our New Man is not a remanufactured Old Man. Old Man "parts" can't pass the kingdom of God quality-control test. Jesus didn't say, "Unless one is dramatically improved, he cannot see the kingdom of God." No. He said, "Unless one is born again, he cannot see the kingdom of God." Our New Man is a new vehicle, a brand-spanking-new person.

As we've seen, our Old Man is sinful, and sin cannot enter Jesus's perfect kingdom. Our old skin is left on the side of the road. We vacate our old house before fully inhabiting our new one. As we discussed in the last chapter, this is an all-in proposition. We can't have it both ways. We can't cling to the old and still inherit the new. We can't simultaneously satisfy the Old Man and the New Man. We can't run two diametrically opposed operating systems. Our New Man download must take over:

> No one can serve two masters. Either you will hate
> the one and love the other, or you will be devoted
> to the one and despise the other. You cannot serve
> both God and money. (Matt. 6:24)

Jesus specifically referred to money in the verse above but also said our hearts are tied to whatever we treasure: "For where your treasure is, there your heart will be also" (Matt. 6:21). Just fill in the blank. "You cannot serve both God and—" Career? Reputation? Golf? Travel? Pleasure? Jesus asks us to be singularly focused on Him and His kingdom: "The eye is the lamp of the body. If your eyes are healthy, your whole body will be full of light" (Matt. 6:22). He wants us to stop living for ourselves and to start living for Him. To submit to His will and purpose for our lives. To run key decisions, choices, and plans by Him.

This sounds really hard for men like us—to give up our former Old Man freedom to become a truly liberated New Man in Christ. Our freedom is the last vestige of who we once were and what we used to serve. This was Peter's temptation too. Jesus said to Peter, on that poignant walk we discussed in the last chapter, "Very truly I tell you, when you were younger you dressed yourself and went where you wanted; but when you are old you will stretch out your hands, and someone else will dress you and lead you where you do not want to go" (John 21:18). John, the author of the gospel of John, said in the next line, "Jesus said this to indicate the kind of death by which Peter would glorify God. Then he said to him, 'Follow me!'"

Peter was crucified in Rome around AD 64–67. He asked to be crucified upside down because he was not worthy to be crucified like his Lord. Peter had learned to give up his own freedom and to feed his Master's sheep. Peter did follow Him, even as far as this cross, where he was pinned down with no means of escape.

Remember my lakefront lawn? The old sod had to be completely killed off before the new seed could be planted. It was the only condition for growth. You might say, "Hey, that's a good deal for someone whose grass is as useless as yours was. But I've got a very attractive 'lawn.' My life has been successful, something to be proud of. I've achieved a great deal. I'm loved and respected. Made something worthwhile out of my days on earth. That's not something to turn over and discard so I can go back to the beginning. If so, what's been the whole point of my life?"

Fair enough. What has been the whole point of your life? That's an awesome question. Go ahead. Enumerate those successes. Write them down. I'm quite certain the list is long. Now, let's review your list. Put a check next to everything you accomplished specifically for and with Jesus in mind. Things you've done with your eyes on God. Be honest. How many items did you check?

I know. You might be annoyed here. This particular challenge could be rubbing you wrong. It sounds unrealistic. Who goes through life thinking like this? Evaluating everything in these terms? Who gets up, goes to work, the hardware store, dry cleaner, car wash, bank, golf club, gym, coffee shop, airport, thinking, *What can I do for Jesus today? How can He use me to make a difference for His kingdom? What lost sheep are in my path today to call or feed?* Certainly not our Old Man. He couldn't care less about Jesus's kingdom. Our Old Man's priorities are elsewhere.

My list got pared down to wallet size when I took a hard look at my life after semiretiring ten years ago. I thought I'd done quite well up to that point, including on the New Man front. Then I looked closer at all that was driving me and what I was living for. I was sobered by what I saw. To put it mildly, I was stripped of my self-deception and shown how much of my Old Man was still in operation. I was ashamed of how much time, energy, talent, and money I'd squandered on my own treasure, in its various forms, up to that point. I wish I could have all those years back, with the New Man eyes through which I now see so much more clearly. Of course, I can't. None of us can.

We can, however, make the rest of our lives the best of our lives—by seeking to live out our remaining years, whatever those may be, with and for Jesus. Operating out of our New Man. Just like Peter did, once he finally got it. That's our journey. That's what this book is all about. Our New Man seed is taking hold, forming good roots, and growing. That New Man download is taking effect. We can delineate him from our Old Man. We're amazed, excited, and maybe a little surprised by how different our New Man's priorities and choices are. *Who is this guy? Who knew I could change so much, become so interested in and focused on working with and for Jesus?* Our Old Man crabgrass scoffs, but we know better. Our New Man lawn is taking over.

What about those good things on our list that we're so proud of and pleased with? Let's place them all at Jesus's feet. Ask Him to make the best of what's good and discard the rest. At the end of the journey, that's what will happen anyway, so it might as well start now. Jesus can be trusted with our treasure in all its forms. He knows us inside and out. Nothing will be lost that ever was worth keeping.

Nineteenth-century English missionary C. T. Studd expressed this best:

Two little lines I heard one day, traveling along life's busy way; Bringing conviction to my heart, and from my mind would not depart;

"Only one life, 'twill soon be past, only what's done for Christ will last."[1]

## GREEN SHOOTS

Tom is a guy who's also about to reevaluate his priorities. He'd been cruising through life in the fast lane. A good guy with great prospects. A life's ambition fulfilled. Now he's hit an unexpected wall and taken an extraordinary detour. One that wasn't in his plan but was in God's. You might be wondering what happens to him after his experience. Let's check in on him.

When he gets out of the car and his feet hit the garage floor, Tom knows he's taken his first step into a new world. Everything seems fresh and different. Clean. Crisp. Pregnant with anticipation. Concerned about how his wife might react, however, he decides to postpone telling her.

The next several weeks are somewhat surreal for Tom. He doesn't discuss his garage experience with anyone, but he can't get it out of his mind. It's as if he's frozen in that moment, going over and over the exact details. He waits for them to dissipate, but they only grow sharper, clearer, more real.

He tries his normal routines at work and at home, but everything he does is now somehow superseded by those images and words. He attempts normal interactions and conversations at work and with Brandy, the kids, and friends but is preoccupied with what's happened to him. He ponders what it all means and what, if anything, he should do about it.

Tom finds it impossible to get back to the man he was before his experience. This is both disconcerting and exhilarating. He knows a change is taking place but isn't sure where it's headed and the implications for the rest of his life. He knows he has to talk to someone. Get it out. Figure it out. He can't go on keeping it inside. He considers calling his friend Ted but decides instead to hit it straight on with Brandy.

This Friday after work, Tom walks into the kitchen from the garage. Brandy greets him: "Hi, honey. How was work?"

Tom chooses his words carefully: "Work was work. To be honest, it's been hard for me to focus there lately."

"Really?" she says. "What's going on?"

Tom's now committed. "Well," he says, "about a month ago, when I got my new car, something unusual happened to me."

Brandy asks him to sit down and takes his hands. She looks pale, as if bracing herself for something. "Exactly what are we talking about?"

Tom sees her concern and tries to put her at ease. "Don't worry. It's nothing bad, and everything's fine with us."

Brandy sighs. "Well, that's a relief. So what's the mystery?"

"This is hard to explain, but … I had an experience with Jesus." Brandy's mouth opens to respond, but Tom holds up his hand. "I know, that sounds strange. Believe me, it was weird for me, too. Everything was fine and normal until I pulled into the garage that day. Then I had some sort of breakdown."

Brandy takes Tom's hands again. "Breakdown? Like a nervous breakdown?"

"Not exactly. No. I just started shaking and crying, and I couldn't move. I tried pulling myself together but couldn't. That's the first time I've ever lost control, lost my bearings."

Brandy squeezes his hands. "Go on, then what?"

"Then I had this experience with Jesus, where He spoke to me and asked me to invite Him into my life." Brandy, wide-eyed, removes her hands. "Jesus spoke that directly to you?"

"Yes, and said more … about my being forgiven."

Brandy smiles. "Well … I guess that can't be all bad." She laughs nervously. "Wow. I wasn't prepared for this. I don't know what to say. This is so unlike you, but I guess it's a good thing."

Tom sees Brandy struggling. Knows she's trying to put on a good face even though she's concerned for what this might all mean. He wants to tell her everything will be back to normal soon. That their life will go on the way it was. But he knows it won't. He has no idea what the future holds now. Only that it will be wonderful. He also knows he loves Brandy more than ever, with a new and more powerful kind of love he doesn't yet understand.

He takes her into his arms. As he holds her close, he silently prays, *Lord, please help her see and understand. I want her in this with me.*

Brandy takes Tom's face in her hands and looks him straight in the eyes. "Honey, I love you," she says. "I've always loved you. You and the kids are my life. I can't say I fully understand what's happened to you, but I think I get it. I believe this is real for you. If it is, we'll both know soon enough. I'm happy for you. Let's just see what's next. This is kind of exciting."

Tom knows Brandy could have gone either way. "I can't tell you how much I appreciate your trust," he says. "I don't underestimate your decision to get in this boat with me. It makes all the difference. I prayed for this."

"You'd better pray the water doesn't get too rough for me. I get seasick."

Tom laughs, gives her another hug, takes her hands. "How about if we do that, pray together?"

Brandy is taken aback. "Now? Here? I guess. Why not?"

Still holding Brandy's hands, Tom begins: "Okay, God. Here we are. Both of us. In this boat with You. This is different. Big-time. I don't know exactly where we're headed, but I do know what happened to me out there in the garage was real. Thanks for helping Brandy understand and come along. I love her with all my heart. Always have. Thanks for bringing her into my life so long ago. Please show us both what's going on and what to do. We're in Your hands. Amen."

Silence. Tom squeezes Brandy's hands, prompting her to pray. He isn't sure if she will. Then she starts: "God. Show us the way. Make me willing. I love this man. Amen."

Tom looks at Brandy. "That was beautiful, honey. Thank you. I love you." They hold each other again, both softly crying, sensing their new journey together.

# SEED SOWERS

Ray and Tom have something in common. Difficult circumstances have driven both to seek God's help. Their marriages and lives are about to shift. Neither of them knows how at this point, but both sense it will be for the better. Little do they know just how much better.

Everyone experiences rough seas at various points in their life: devastating illnesses, untimely deaths of loved ones, job losses, financial reversals, marital and relationship issues, divorces, break-ups, and breaches. These all take their toll but are also more likely than favorable events to bring people to God.

Men like us can make a difference in those lives. Despite Tom's discomfort with and resistance to him, Ted was likely a game changer in Tom's decision to turn to God. Carmen entered Ray and Birgit's lives and, with God's direction, seems ready to help them sort things out. Has someone made that difference in your life? Perhaps someone is even now. In whose life might you be used by God to make that critical difference, now or in the future?

We're exploring the possibility of a dramatically different purpose for living. Examining and weighing Jesus's desire for us to get to know Him, turn our lives over, bear His fruit, be witnesses to the reality of His presence, and share His words of life with those around us—point and lead them to Him. There's a reason we're here. Called to something bigger than ourselves, something eternal. If we hear Jesus's call, take on the New Man, follow Him, begin living for Him, and stay the course, we'll look around and ask, "What about him, or her, or him? Am I part of God's plan for them?" Our longing for them to know the New Man life we've discovered comes from the Holy Spirit within us. That makes us New Man—seed sowers, water givers, and fertilizers in their lives.

Jesus told Nicodemus, "The wind blows wherever it pleases. You hear its sound, but you cannot tell where it comes from or where it is going. So it is with everyone born of the Spirit" (John 3:8). I love this image of God's Spirit blowing into people's lives without them necessarily even knowing who just showed up or through whom He came. His voice, spoken to men. He wants everyone to hear the words He spoke through His son, Jesus. And has continued to speak through His disciples for two thousand years.

The first disciples were filled with the Holy Spirit to carry Jesus's words of life throughout the known world. The "sound" of the Spirit was heard through them. One couldn't see the Spirit. People met Him through the disciples. They were His carriers, His vessels, His voice, His sound.

That distribution model hasn't changed. The Holy Spirit is carried (blown) everywhere (like the wind) through Jesus's modern-day disciples. Through people like us. We may have heard His voice from a pulpit, through a friend who shared Jesus's words of life with us in person, or from a book, music, television, radio, another medium, or all of the above. I heard through the young woman who would eventually become my wife. I'm quite certain there were others before her.

The work of the Spirit, through the committed cadre of New Men and Women, is the same yesterday, today, and tomorrow: "So it is with everyone born of the Spirit." There is nothing more exciting and fulfilling.

Tom, Brandy, Ray, and Birgit are all about to have their life plans and perspectives changed. God has shown up and rocked their worlds in unexpected ways. For the moment, their paths forward are unclear. We sense, however, that they're on good footing in rich soil, that the new shoots coming up are far healthier than the ones they're replacing. We'll follow their stories in the next chapter.

Maybe God is also about to grow your shoots to levels you never imagined. Are you ready?

Let's discuss the New Man/New Life questions we've been considering in this chapter and see where you stand.

1. Can you relate to the "Footprints in the Sand" story? Have you felt carried by God?

2. Have you had an extraordinary experience that convinced you God was involved in your life or had your faith encouraged when you were in need of confirmation of His presence? Starter fertilizer, so to speak? If so, what was that?

3. What do Tom and Ray have in common in this chapter? What's different?

4. Can you relate, on any level, to either Tom or Ray? If so, how?

5. What, if anything, do Brandy and Birgit have in common?

6. How would your wife have reacted in Brandy's and Birgit's situations? Consider asking her.

7. Can you think of other "masters," besides God, that you serve? What are they?

8. What was your response to the "whole point of your life" exercise?

9. Did it change your perspective on your definition of success? How?

10. Has your view of your purpose and passion changed during this journey? How?

# NOTES

1. Quoted in Billy Graham, *Till Armageddon* (Waco, TX: Word Books, 1981), 198.

# NEW SUIT

Our New Man longs to be clothed in the heavenly
suit God has tailor-made for him.

Our journey thus far has provided us with a close look at a special job offer and with the opportunity to evaluate our desire and willingness to take it on. Not a trivial matter when we realize that the position of New Man offered by God is a full-time occupation. It's not open to negotiation and equivocation.

This job is not like what we do or did to make money. Most of us consciously or subconsciously put off serious commitment to spiritual "work" to a time when we believe we'll be better able to focus "there." This is the wrong way to think about the job of living out our faith. It reflects the misguided notion that giving our lives to God and serving Him is like a normal, time-boxed profession.

As we've learned, our New Man isn't constrained by time. His higher nature engages every area of our life, all the time. There's no church/sacred time on one day and world/secular time the rest of the week. No double-minded, halfhearted Christians here. Whether we're unemployed, still working, fully retired, or somewhere in between, the life we now live gets acquired and assimilated by our new boss, Jesus, and becomes imbued with His purpose and governance:

> Whatever you do, work at it with all your heart, as working for the Lord, not for human masters, since you know that you will receive an inheritance from the Lord as a reward. It is the Lord Christ you are serving. (Col. 3:23–24)

The everyday logistics of our lives usually don't change. But with our new operating system, our purpose for living, doing, and relating changes because we're now seed sowers and fruit bearers for God, aligning our interests to His.

Some of us signed on for the New Man position years ago and stayed the course, albeit with a few detours. Others started out well but forgot or went AWOL and now want to reengage at a more substantive level. Others have understood and accepted the job during this journey. Many are still weighing options. A few have declined the offer. It's just not for them. A lot are still on the fence. God's offer is, of course, always on the table, but there's not a flood of applications. Jesus is looking for men willing to follow Him:

> Then he [Jesus] said to his disciples, "The harvest is plentiful but the workers are few. Ask the Lord of the harvest, therefore, to send out workers into his harvest field." (Matt. 9:37–38)

## IF THE SUIT FITS

How does the ephemeral piece of real estate known as our body, this matter that carries around our spirit, fit into the New Man position we're discussing? No matter what we've ever thought about our bodies, it's likely to be quite different from the New Man perspective provided by Paul and explored here:

> For we know that if the earthly tent we live in is destroyed, we have a building from God, an eternal house in heaven, not built by human hands. Meanwhile we groan, longing to be clothed instead with our heavenly dwelling, because when we are clothed, we will not be found naked. For while we are in this tent, we groan and are burdened, because we do not wish to be unclothed but to be clothed instead with our heavenly dwelling, so that what is mortal may be swallowed up by life. Now the one who has fashioned us for this very purpose is God,

who has given us the Spirit as a deposit, guarantee-
ing what is to come. (2 Cor. 5:1–5)

Did you get that? Let me suggest an explanation of what I think
Paul was saying here. If we're born again, when our earthly body
gives out, our New Man (temporarily housed in our earthly body)
takes on a new body that God has crafted for him. It's a spiritual
body like God has, tailor-made for the heavenly house we'll inhabit
for eternity. The new spiritual body is our heavenly clothing, so to
speak. But our New Man still works, with the help of the Spirit,
within the constraints of our earthly body.

Remember our "new house" analogy? You sell your current house
but rent it back until your new house is complete. As your new house
is being built, you begin occupying it. You spend more and more
time there, until you've completely moved out of the rented house.
It's an easy transition. So it is for the Christian. When he dies, he
leaves his tent with its wear and tear and enters an eternal dwelling
where there is no mutability or mortality. If we refer to Paul's clothing analogy, our tailor (the Holy Spirit) has taken our measurements
and fit us for a new suit. That suit has already been bought and paid
for. All we have to do is pick it up for that great trip.

This isn't how most of us think about our body, yet Paul's is the
attitude we're supposed to adopt. For him, his earthly body was a
vehicle for his New Man work on earth. Nothing more.

Paul was right. Our New Man journey is about investing our
mental, emotional, and physical treasure wisely. We shouldn't be dis-
proportionately focused on our earthly body, as if that was the be-all
and end-all, nor think that when it stops, we stop. As hard as we may

try for "heaven on earth," that's not going to happen. Our bodies will eventually wear out. Many of you are painfully aware of that now. Our life here is temporary. Our permanent home and life in heaven are eternal. Our New Man will move out of one and into the other. The New Man's future bears an immortal body and wears a new suit.

To be clear, I'm in no way suggesting that we shouldn't take care of our earthly bodies. Paul spoke to that too: "Do you not know that your bodies are temples of the Holy Spirit, who is in you, whom you have received from God? You are not your own; you were bought at a price. Therefore honor God with your bodies" (1 Cor. 6:19–20). But Paul also put the body in perspective: "For physical training is of some value, but godliness has value for all things, holding promise for both the present life and the life to come" (1 Tim. 4:8).

Honoring God with our bodies entails properly maintaining them, with commonsense healthcare practices, as well as submitting them to God for His purposes. Respecting what we do with them—ensuring, to the best of our ability and within our control, that the "tent" for our New Man work on earth remains in good condition *and* glorifies God. Our body for His work. This is the New Man attitude.

## REPLACING OLD MAN REFLEXES

Figuratively speaking, our New Man "groans" (longs) to be "clothed" (equipped) for work here, so as not to be found "naked" (wanting) there. I believe that's what Paul was referring to when he said, "So that what is mortal may be swallowed up by life." Think of this as the process of the Spirit fitting us for our New Man suit. The tailoring is gradual and takes place here in our earthly body. By the time we're ready for our trip, we're comfortable in our new heavenly clothes.

I love this image. It helps me focus on what's important. Given the choice of showing up in heaven in a fine-looking suit and tie, properly dressed for that great occasion, or in ragged shorts and a dirty T-shirt, I'll take the suit. So how can I influence that outcome? How can we? By outgrowing our old clothes. I'll explain.

Before our decision to be born again of the Spirit, as we've come to understand that, our earthly body was the exclusive property of our earth-born Old Man. He ruled the house (our body) before the Spirit-birth of our New Man. Not surprisingly, our earthly body is loaded with the memory reflexes associated with the lower nature attitudes, priorities, and values that control and drive our old operating system, our Old Man. As we learned in chapter seven, the process by which our New Man nature and priorities become dominant is gradual. Our Old Man is ultimately no contest for our New Man. Just as that snake's dead skin doesn't peel off easily, however, neither do our Old Man reflexes.

Here's an example. I have a semiretired friend I'll call Carl who's mature and strong in his New Man development. He was prominent and highly regarded in the world of investment banking. A partner in a prestigious firm at an early age, his star kept rising. He loved the hunt and took pride in negotiating and pulling off successful deals. This is a world, however, where yesterday's successes have a short shelf life and "stars" are soon forgotten. That world doesn't recognize Carl the way it used to. When at the top of his game, he'd have been quick to say that his true identity was not in his worldly position. But dropping his former identity after semiretirement was a harder battle than he thought it would be. For quite a while, before becoming more firmly established in his New Man identity and purpose, his instinct in social situations was to remind everyone of his former titles and accomplishments. I suspect he's still not entirely immune from that urge.

I think we've all experienced a bit of that. The earthly body and mind-set constantly remind us of the life we used to live that was driven by our lower nature. As we pursue the New Man job to which Jesus calls us, those Old Man memory reflexes are gradually replaced and eventually wiped out. Without the Holy Spirit living inside of us, the Old Man would never cede real estate. If we're born again, our New Man is fully capable of and equipped by God to overcome our old, unredeemed attitudes and habits: "You, dear children, are from God and have overcome them, because the one who is in you is greater than the one who is in the world" (1 John 4:4). We simply need to be willing to give these up and to replace them with our New Man attitudes, priorities, and values. Paul's description of this exchange says it all:

> Since, then, you have been raised with Christ, set your hearts on things above, where Christ is, seated at the right hand of God. Set your minds on things above, not on earthly things. For you died, and your life is now hidden with Christ in God. When Christ, who is your life, appears, then you also will appear with him in glory.

Put to death, therefore, whatever belongs to your earthly nature: sexual immorality, impurity, lust, evil desires and greed, which is idolatry. Because of these, the wrath of God is coming. You used to walk in these ways, in the life you once lived. But now you must also rid yourselves of all such things as these: anger, rage, malice, slander, and filthy language from your lips. Do not lie to each other, since you have taken off your old self with its practices and have put on the new self, which is being renewed in knowledge in the image of its Creator. Here there is no Gentile or Jew, circumcised or uncircumcised, barbarian, Scythian, slave or free, but Christ is all, and is in all.

Therefore, as God's chosen people, holy and dearly loved, clothe yourselves with compassion, kindness, humility, gentleness and patience. Bear with each other and forgive one another if any of you has a grievance against someone. Forgive as the Lord forgave you. And over all these virtues put on love, which binds them all together in perfect unity. (Col. 3:1–14)

Giving up Old Man attitudes and habits in this process is easier said than done. There are many to be displaced, and we guys have most of the big ones in common. For example, that familiar drive for food, shelter, and clothing. In varying degrees, our Old Man concerns himself with building up a sufficient storehouse to handle the worst of circumstances. He becomes preoccupied with ways of strengthening his financial position. Nothing is quite enough. He never knows what might come. He plans and plans. Even when he achieves his objective, he still feels exposed, so he continues to plan and protect. This cycle doesn't end until after we're born again and a new perspective takes over.

Our friend Tom is about to have a major breakthrough in this area.

## BREAKING THE CYCLE

Tom had always been driven by a powerful desire to accumulate wealth. Ego gratification and the social circles into which that gave him access were less important to him than the money itself. Money meant security and freedom. He had a twofold objective: make and conservatively invest enough so that he and Brandy could retire comfortably at sixty and leave a meaningful, tax-protected estate behind for their children and grandchildren. He'd already achieved the first objective. The next five years would go toward the second.

After years of hard work, Tom and Brandy could now make almost any monetary choice they wanted to. "Can we afford this?" became a question of their past. They'd graduated into the select world of "What do we want to do?" Yet they never forgot their modest roots. They'd worked for their money honestly and graciously accepted the responsibilities that came with it. They were generous to local charities and to school and community fundraisers. They overpaid those who did their household and grounds chores and maintenance. They were, on balance, modest about their wealth while taking an "appropriate" degree of pride in their accomplishments.

Tom's salary and bonuses had far exceeded the family expenses for years. He was able to max out his IRA and put most of his bonuses into savings. The resulting nest egg was significant, as was the asset of their Greenwich home. About half his wealth was in the value of the shares he held in the investment firm in which he was now a full partner. While that was a lot to have in one asset, he knew it was secure. The private firm had been in existence for nearly fifty years and was one of the most respected in its areas of alternative investing. They had a blue-chip client base that expected and received respectable returns on relatively conservative trades. The firm's policy was for retiring partners to sell their shares back to the remaining partners at current valuations. Tom's shares had gone up tenfold in value over the years, even after the 2008–9 market meltdown. Considering the firm's earnings-growth rate, his shares would likely double over the next five years. He had that dollar amount firmly engraved in his mind. It might end up a little lower or higher, but it would be close.

Thoughts of the firm, career, and financial security had dominated many of Tom's waking hours for years. Since his conversion experience a month ago, however, these all seemed to fade into the background. When he woke up early this particular Monday morning for work, he thought about calling in sick. He and Brandy had spent the rest of the weekend going over the details of his experience and trying to figure it all out. He now wanted to spend the day with her. Take more time to talk and think. Try to connect with Ted. He knew, however, that he needed to face the reality of his office.

The workday on Friday had been a little unusual. The two senior partners who were frequently on the trading floor where Tom and his team worked were sequestered in an office together. When Tom went to lunch, he noticed several visitors he didn't recognize. When he arrives back at the office this Monday morning, all the other partners are already there. Another anomaly. He's usually the first one in. As he walks to his office, he tries connecting the dots. Is something going on with the firm? He approaches his office and greets Maria, his secretary.

"Hi, Tom," she says. "All the partners are in the conference room. They'd like you to join them."

Now he's concerned. "What's up? Why all the mystery?"

She looks at him and shrugs her shoulders. "Would you like a coffee before you go in?"

"Nope. I'm good. Thanks. Let's see what's happening." As he moves toward the conference room, a wave of fear comes over him. He says a silent prayer as he walks: *Hey, Jesus, are You still here? I don't have a good feeling. Please go in there with me.*

When he enters, all conversation stops. One of the senior partners, Craig Morrison, stands up and points to a seat. No other greetings or handshakes. "Have a seat, Tom."

Tom pauses to glance at the other partners. All eyes are down. "Sure. Did somebody die?" He laughs. They don't.

Tom sits down and looks around the table. These are his partners. People he's known and worked with for years. Friends and colleagues. They now look like pallbearers at his funeral. He says another prayer: *Help me out here, Jesus.*

Craig begins. "Tom ... we have a problem." The silence seems to linger for minutes.

"What kind of problem?"

Kevin Jamison, the other senior partner, takes over. "A big one. Last Thursday, your team bet against Populace Bancorp."

A bell goes off in Tom's head. "Right. So?"

"So, the bet was wrong. They paid out their dividend in full late Friday. You'd already left the office. The hedge was twenty million."

Tom feels like he's been shot with a stun gun. He's never been involved in a mistake of this magnitude. He goes numb. All eyes are on him.

"Twenty million? How can that be? Our limit is ten, which is what I approved."

Craig shoots back. "Right. This was for twenty! The damage is done. We've been sitting here trying to figure out how to tell our clients. We've exceeded our limits. They won't absorb the loss. The firm is liable. Our insurance might not cover a lawsuit because of the breach. We're checking with legal."

Tom's face is ashen. "This is horrific. I never authorized twenty. I had no idea. It must have been an administrative mistake in the trade."

"We've already looked into that," Kevin says. "It wasn't an error. You should have been watching your team more closely."

Kevin takes off his glasses and puts his elbows on the table, hands folded. "As bad as that is, it's not our only problem."

Tom takes in the whole room to make sure he isn't having a nightmare. He's watching a train wreck in slow motion. "Not our only problem? How long have you guys been here?" He sees he's on the witness stand.

Kevin leans into the table. "We've been here awhile. It seems there've been irregularities with one of your team member's trades over the past month. But nothing on a scale like this."

Tom feels like he's shrinking. He thinks about the garage. Brandy. *This can't be happening.* "Who? What irregularities?"

Kevin continues. "Small ones. All related to regional bank bonds. Our audit team didn't pick anything up, but we got an unexpected visit from a couple of SEC folks on Friday. Just a preliminary inquiry. They asked us to check it out and get back to them. It appears that Frank D'Stefano has been right on eighteen out of twenty swaps in the past three weeks. All regionals. He made the Populace trade too."

Frank was one of Tom's best performers. A twenty-eight-year-old MIT whiz kid he'd hired right out of school. Made lots of money for Tom's clients and the firm. Quiet. First in, last out every day. Never a hint of any issues. Tom had authorized Frank to make the ten-million Populace trade on Thursday. Tom had asked, "What's our probability? That ten-million is our limit." Frank had answered confidently: "Considering their mark-to-market, I've calculated a 5 percent chance they'll pay out a dividend tomorrow." Tom wasn't entirely comfortable but gave the go-ahead based on Frank's history. This wasn't a business of perfect odds. "Go for it," he'd said. "Be right!"

"Okay," Tom says. "I know Frank's on a good run, but I wouldn't suspect him of inside trading. The twenty million is another story. I'll get with him immediately. Let's meet back here in an hour. We'll figure this out together."

"It's not that simple, Tom," Craig nearly shouts. "We're looking at a *tsunami* here! A twenty-million loss coupled with an SEC investigation. Even if Frank ends up innocent, he intentionally doubled up on Populace. An unprecedented violation of our client covenants that will need to be explained."

Kevin takes over again, calmly. "We already met with him over the weekend, confirmed the breach, got Legal and HR involved, and terminated him for cause. He's gone."

Tom protests. "You fired him over the weekend? Why wasn't I informed and included?"

Kevin stands up. He's obviously been rehearsed. "Tom, we're all your friends here. You've been a huge part of our firm's success ever since you joined us thirty years ago. You've done well, and so have we." All heads are nodding in agreement. "However, we've hit a serious iceberg. We now believe Frank may very well have had inside knowledge at most of the regional banks he's been trading. We haven't yet disclosed that to the SEC but will have to soon. If he's charged and found guilty, it will be hard to keep many of our major clients. They'll be demanding a return of their Populace loss in either case. We could end up fighting for our lives. We've been discussing this all weekend and since early this morning. The best course for damage control at the moment is to distance the firm from Frank's activities. So, we've all concluded that we need to ask you to resign, effective today."

Tom feels like he is watching a movie of someone else's life rather than his own. The reality hasn't fully settled in. He says nothing.

"We hate having to do this," Kevin says, "and it's possible we might survive with you still here, but we simply can't take that chance. This isn't a termination, unless of course you decide not to accept our request for your resignation. Naturally, we'll honor the partner agreement to buy your shares. However, as you know, the agreement allows for up to six months to settle on a valuation of your shares. There's no way of telling what they'll be worth by the time this whole ordeal shakes out. We all carry the same fate on that front."

Craig interjects, "Let's hope there's still a firm with shares to buy. We've all seen firms our size sink like stones once things like this get out."

Tom doesn't speak for nearly fifteen seconds. You can hear a pin drop. He finally collects himself and looks at all the partners, one by one. "Did you all agree to my termination, call it what you will?" Each nods yes. "Then I guess there's nothing more to discuss." He looks at Kevin. "May I have until the end of the week to think this over? To make certain resignation is my best option?"

"We thought you might need a couple days," Kevin says. "Let's make it end of day Wednesday."

Tom remains calm. He gets up and turns to leave the room. Jeremy Christof, a partner peer to Tom and close friend since grad school at Wharton, stands and extends his hand. "I'm sorry about this, buddy. Believe me, it kills us all to do this."

Tom considers brushing him off and giving some choice words to the senior partners, but something inside says to take Jeremy's hand. "I know. No matter what, I'll be fine. Something more important than this happened to me recently. While you were all planning my termination, someone else has been tending to my salvation. I'll tell you all about it another time. I'll see you Wednesday."

At that, each partner stands up, some clearly puzzled by Tom's "salvation" comment. They let it go and shake his hand. Jeremy hugs him on his way out. He accepts their good wishes but knows it isn't over.

Tom's ride home seems like the end of a chapter that began when he pulled out of the Mercedes dealership a month earlier. *How bizarre*, he thinks to himself, *that my life has been so completely turned upside down in such a short period. From everything's perfect to a perfect storm. Situations like this don't happen to guys like me. Yet here I am!*

He carefully thinks through his options for a worst-case scenario. *Our lifestyle will have to change. There'll be some embarrassment and explanation to friends, but that won't be a big deal. Maybe for Brandy. Brandy! This won't go down well with her. Her heart's set on Jupiter Island and Nantucket. But I think she'll be okay as long as we're together. Not the plan, but not all bad. Why am I feeling so good ... free? Hey, Jesus ... did You see this bullet coming?*

## LETTING OUT THE SEAMS

Tom has had no reason to be concerned for his and his family's physical well-being for years—until now. But this is big. It changes everything. How will he handle it? We can see that he's off to a good start, but will he stay the course?

Our New Man understands his role and purpose here and God's interest and involvement in providing when we're focused on honoring, glorifying, and serving Him.

A military analogy comes to mind. Those whose job is to serve their country in the armed forces rely on the good-faith promise of their employer, the government, to provide their basic necessities. Jesus doesn't leave His followers destitute nor does He want them to worry:

Therefore I tell you, do not worry about your life, what you will eat or drink; or about your body, what you will wear. Is not life more than food, and the body more than clothes? Look at the birds of the air; they do not sow or reap or store away in barns, and yet your heavenly Father feeds them. Are you not much more valuable than they? Can any one of you by worrying add a single hour to your life?

And why do you worry about clothes? See how the flowers of the field grow. They do not labor or spin. Yet I tell you that not even Solomon in all his splendor was dressed like one of these. If that is how God clothes the grass of the field, which is here today and tomorrow is thrown into the fire, will he not much more clothe you—you of little faith? So do not worry, saying, "What shall we eat?" or "What shall we drink?" or "What shall we wear?" For the pagans run after all these things, and your heavenly Father knows that you need them. But seek first his kingdom and his righteousness, and all these things will be given to you as well. Therefore do not worry about tomorrow, for tomorrow will worry about itself. Each day has enough trouble of its own. (Matt. 6:25–34)

Notice the condition for provision: "Seek first his kingdom and his righteousness." Who wouldn't want this kind of ultimate insurance? Who wouldn't want to be free from anxiety, regardless of how much we have or don't have? Our Old Man wouldn't. He isn't aligned to God's kingdom and righteousness. Our New Man gets this principle and is at peace and satisfied with the terms. He doesn't need to strive for more protection and security because his life here is in balance. As we become more familiar and comfortable with this New Man truth, our anxiety-driven Old Man reflexes begin to dissipate. Our attitude toward work and money change. This is one of the areas, a major one, in which the Holy Spirit works to fit us for our New Man suit. Paul is a great example of one whose attitude toward money and his earthly job of tent making were aligned to his New Man purpose:

> I have learned to be content whatever the circum-
> stances. I know what it is to be in need, and I know
> what it is to have plenty. I have learned the secret of
> being content in any and every situation, whether
> well fed or hungry, whether living in plenty or in
> want. I can do all this through him who gives me
> strength. (Phil. 4:11–13)

As our New Man grows in strength and begins to occupy more space in our earthly body, the Old Man's reflexes have less hold on him. This process is akin to letting out the seams of our earthly body to make room for our heavenly one, our new suit. If we're born again, our body becomes a temple of the Holy Spirit, bought at a price and suitable for His work in and through us. Therefore we should always, in everything, seek to honor Him with our earthly tent.

What agreement is there between the temple of God and idols? For we are the temple of the living God. As God has said:

"I will live with them
  and walk among them,
and I will be their God,
  and they will be my people." (2 Cor. 6:16)

In this chapter we've been looking into the possibility of a whole new "wardrobe"—one more appropriate for our New Man Journey, tailor-made by God. Let's review some related questions.

1. Before this chapter, had you ever considered being a Christian a job?

2. In the context of the New Man, what's the purpose of our earthly body?

3. What was Paul's attitude toward his heavenly body?

4. What did Paul mean by not wanting to arrive "naked" at his "heavenly dwelling"?

5. Which Old Man "memory reflexes" do you find to be most persistent in your life?

6. What's the best prescription for overcoming Old Man habits?

7. Why is Tom feeling so good after being forced by his partners to resign?

8. How would you handle his situation?

# 10

# ULTIMATE VICTORY

Stay fixed on heaven—it's where you're headed.

Most of us have thought about, planned for, and worked toward the goal of enjoying our final phase of life. We've dreamed, in one form or another, about a time and place to live out our golden years in peace and comfort.

The New Man Journey is no threat to our retirement dream. It is, in fact, the one sure thing we can count on to make the highest and best parts of our dream a reality. Our retirement years are a perfect fit for the New Man clothes we're now wearing or are about to put on. These clothes radiate the nature and presence of Jesus and point others toward Him. They provide light, wisdom, and healing to those we love and to strangers in need of His words of life and hope:

> Therefore, as God's chosen people, holy and dearly
> loved, clothe yourselves with compassion, kindness,
> humility, gentleness and patience…. And over all
> these virtues put on love, which binds them all
> together in perfect unity. (Col. 3:12, 14)

Tom, Brandy, Ray, and Birgit are on their way to retirement lives that are very different from the ones they'd planned. Ones where the Lord, rather than themselves, will be at the center.

## WE'VE ONLY BEGUN TO SEE

Ray and Birgit met for lunch as planned on Monday with Carmen and her husband, Glen. They chose a pleasant spot in La Jolla, suggested by Birgit.

Carmen and Glen were well prepared. They knew it was a "divine appointment" and that their job was to share their story and let the Lord take it where He wanted. They prayed for the upcoming lunch all weekend and had their Bible study group pray in church the day before the lunch. It was a beautiful autumn day as they sat outside overlooking the rocky coast.

Carmen wasted no time in telling Ray and Birgit how excited she was to be with them again and to explore what

God was doing in their lives. Subtlety wasn't her style. Ray and Birgit knew a major shift in their lives was taking place that somehow involved God, but they couldn't put their finger on what it was. God had creatively supplied Carmen and Glen to fill out the picture and provide the road map. They listened intently as Carmen described her abusive childhood and mistrust of men, the toll that had taken on her marriage to Glen, their turning to God, and the subsequent miraculous turnaround.

After some discussion, Carmen asked Ray and Birgit if they wanted to turn their marriage over to God too. Ray and Birgit were disarmed by the innocence of her question. They were in a public setting, yet to Ray and Birgit, it was as if no one else was around and this was the only matter in the world that counted.

They looked at each other, saw the softness and tears in each other's eyes, looked back at Carmen and Glen, and nodded their heads yes. The four of them held hands. Their waiter could see something was going on and gave them space. Others looked over with curiosity and then continued their own conversations. Ray prayed first.

"Lord, please come into my life ... our lives ... and our marriage. Take over our future. Thank You. Amen."

Birgit's prayer was more elaborate.

"Lord, I can't believe we're doing this." All laughed a little. "I'm sorry I left You so long ago. I've always known You were there with me, even though I wasn't with You. That was so dumb of me. I can only imagine how different my life might have been if I'd chosen to stay with You. I'm so ashamed. Anyway, I'm here now with Ray, my husband, who I love. Thank You for him. For giving him to me. Thank You for Carmen and Glen. For giving them to us. Thank You for coming into my life and our lives. Yes, we invite You. In Jesus's name, amen."

After their prayer, Ray asked Carmen and Glen, "So, what do we do now?"

"Now," Carmen said, "you begin living for the Lord."

Ray asked the obvious: "What does that mean?"

"Just ask Him," Glen said. "He'll show you."

Ray and Birgit did ask, and they were shown. Carmen and Glen introduced them to new friends who helped prepare them for the job the Lord had for them.

They never followed through on the motor home idea. The journey on which they embarked together in La Jolla was a far better solution for their marriage and started them on a much more interesting journey.

They stayed in their house in the golf community for twenty-one years until moving into a smaller place near one of their kids. The routine they'd begun after retiring didn't change, with one major exception—their purpose for it all. After lunch that day in La Jolla, nothing could ever be the same. Ray and Birgit had come to a crossroad and knew it.

It's been twenty-seven years since Ray and Birgit started their new life together. Now in their mideighties, they can't imagine their marriage without Christ at the center.

Ray has come to discover that the boredom he experienced with Birgit was a result of looking to her for something that can be found only in an intimate relationship with the Lord. He refers to his rebirth as the "gift that keeps on giving." The closer he comes to the Lord, the more his love for and enjoyment of Birgit grows.

Birgit has realized that her ultimate security isn't in Ray, her family, or her ability to fend for herself. She's transferred her dependency to the Lord and become stronger as a person than she ever thought possible.

The job the Lord ended up giving Ray and Birgit has been to share their discovery of the Lord with hundreds of men and women over the years and to take retirement couples "under their wing," as they put it. To help them transform their "old-age" marriages into the regenerated and exciting relationships still possible with the Lord.

Sometimes, when Ray's counseling a friend or he and Birgit are advising a couple, he sees the loving eyes of those sheep from his long ago dream and knows that he's fulfilling his purpose.

Every year, Ray and Birgit go to lunch at the same location in La Jolla on their "new-birth anniversary," as they've come to describe that day. The restaurant has changed hands several times, but the memory of it is as fresh and real as it was so long ago when they prayed together with Carmen and Glen to receive Christ.

They have a little ritual. Ray raises his glass and asks, "How can we still be so interested in each other after all these years? So much in love?" He always receives the same response from Birgit:

"Because we've only begun to see the depth of who we are in Christ."

We've only begun to see, indeed! Birgit's answer is the best summary of the New Man Journey. Our New Man is formed in His image, with His DNA, His operating system. Can we even begin to imagine the height, depth, breadth, and width of Christ? Of course not. The New Man miracle is that when we're born again we are given His nature, clothed with the fullness of His Spirit, aligned to His kingdom. We share in the inexhaustible riches of His attributes. Our Old Man knows only the tiny chink of his own reality. Our New Man knows the fullness of God through His Son, Jesus Christ.

Ray and Birgit have tapped into that fullness and discovered the treasure-house within each other. Their lives and relationships have been regenerated and transformed, as have been those of countless individuals and couples like them over the millennia since Jesus's ultimate victory.

Tom and Brandy are another case in point.

## THE SOUND OF BAGPIPES

After his termination, Tom kept waiting for the reality of his work situation to dawn on him and for the fear to take over. That never happened. He also considered hiring an attorney to fight his termination but began seeing his circumstances more as a blessing than a curse and decided not to fight his partners' decision. Instead, he turned the financial outcome over to the Lord. *He'll be a better Advocate than any I could hire,* he said to himself.

His heart was light the whole way home that Monday of his termination. He sensed God's hand in his unforeseen freedom from work. He had an excitement about what might come next.

Brandy handled the news better than he'd expected. When he asked why she was taking everything so well, she told him she couldn't explain it but that the change she saw in him and their prayer together had something to do with it.

Tom and Ted connected a couple of days later. Ted had a business proposition he wanted to discuss. The last thing he expected to hear was the news about Tom's garage conversion and his Monday morning termination. They didn't get to the business conversation. Ted told Tom that he and Katie had agreed a year ago to pray daily for him and Brandy, to pray that they'd both come to the Lord and that their friendship might be restored.

Ted invited Tom to join a men's Bible study group at his church. Tom accepted. Katie asked Brandy to come to a women's community Bible study in Greenwich. Over the next year, Tom and Brandy's social life gradually incorporated friendships they'd made in their Bible study groups. They started attending Ted and Katie's church and eventually became members.

Tom's former firm was able to survive, but not without a huge haircut. Tom received a modest payout—enough on which to retire, but only with significant adjustments. They were able to get a decent price for their big home in Greenwich and find a small one in nearby Cos Cob. They decided to stay there where the kids had grown up and they could be near their new church and Christian friends. Tom volunteered to set up a class on money and investing for young couples in their church. Brandy got involved with the leadership of community Bible study.

Tom and Brandy's relationship with Ted and Katie grew into a special one over the years that followed. They confided in each other and prayed with and for one another through good and difficult times. Those didn't preclude growing pains, relationship setbacks, health challenges, and a few family crises. When Katie contracted breast cancer and Tom and Brandy's daughter was almost killed in a rafting accident in Colorado, they were the rocks on whom they mutually leaned.

Tom and Brandy celebrated their fiftieth wedding anniversary at their Cos Cob home with their children, grandchildren, Ted, Katie, and their family. After dinner, Ted made a toast:

"To our best friends, Tom and Brandy, and to their family and our family gathered here tonight. Who would have known and who could have predicted that the great young couple we met so many years ago would end up becoming the ones with whom we'd travel this remarkable road. I guess we could have done it without you … and almost did." Everyone laughed. "But it's been so much better with you. Our lives have been enriched by yours. We've watched you change from the young people you were to the strong individuals and couple in Christ you've become. We're proud of you. Of the way you've stayed the course and are finishing the race well. We love you both. Let's all do this again … on your sixtieth."

They all toasted, laughed, hugged, and agreed. However, there was no sixtieth for Tom and Brandy. Three years later, Tom set off on a walk on a favorite trail in the Mianus River park near their home. It was a beautiful early June morning. The tulips were in full bloom. Tom had grown to love his special "quiet times with the Lord in the park," as he referred to them. He would talk and listen to Him while he walked. About anything and everything. It was just a time for getting closer. He'd finish this routine by sitting at the foot of a favorite hemlock. A stately old man on the bank of the river. There he'd take out his well-worn friend—a pocket-sized New Testament and Psalms—and pick up where he'd left off from his last devotional reading.

This time was different.

Tom reads from the fifteenth chapter of 1 Corinthians, where Paul deals with the resurrection of the body and concludes with, "Therefore, my dear brothers and sisters, stand firm. Let nothing move you. Always give yourselves fully to the work of the Lord, because you know that your labor in the Lord is not in vain."

As he finishes reading, Tom feels unusually dizzy. He leans back against the tree. He knows that at age seventy-eight, it could be anything.

"Lord, I'm feeling kind of strange," he prays. "Not sure what's happening, and I'm a little frightened here. Please help me through this." He feels the Lord's presence in a particularly strong way. The dizziness abates. He senses the Lord directing him to Psalm 116:15. He opens his Bible to the passage and reads it aloud: "Precious in the sight of the LORD is the death of his faithful servants."

Tom connects the passage with what he just read and knows this means something. "Am I dying here, Lord? Is this my time? I'm not sure I'm ready. What about Brandy? We're old. She needs me."

Tom is flooded with love for Brandy and an assurance that everything is exactly the way it is supposed to be.

Suddenly everything turns a bright white. He feels as if he's being pulled out of his body. Higher and higher. Over the top of the old hemlock and above Long Island Sound. As he drifts, time seems to stand still. He sees a small boat on the sound. He looks closely and sees himself in the boat as a younger man. He understands. His new life began in that boat with the Lord, twenty-three years earlier, and it is continuing with Him now. Tom is overjoyed at the prospect of the next phase of his journey but is still concerned about Brandy. "Lord, can I speak with her first?" he asks.

Tom hears a shout from heaven: "I am making everything new!"

He turns toward the voice. Overwhelmed by the intensity of light and color, he has to look away. He sees his still body below, against the hemlock. He's being pulled back. Then all goes blank.

The next thing he sees is Brandy looking over him, holding his hand.

A jogger found Tom, leaning against the hemlock, unconscious. When the paramedics arrived, they were barely able to get a pulse, but he was still alive and was immediately put on life support upon arrival at the Greenwich Hospital emergency room. He'd suffered a severe cerebral aneurysm.

Tom's death was quick and painless. Brandy, their son, Brent, their daughter, Kelly, and Ted and Katie were all with him in the critical care unit, where he'd been in a coma for two days. Something unusual occurred at the moment of his passing. As Brandy stood over Tom, holding his hand, he suddenly came out of the coma, sat up, took Brandy's face in his hands, looked her straight in the eyes, and softly said, "It's everything and more Brandy … so much more." With that, he laid back down. The life support machines announced his transition. Brandy held him, knew he was gone. Silent tears. You could hear a pin drop. Brandy was certain she heard the faint sound of bagpipes.

## SOWN PERISHABLE, RAISED IMPERISHABLE

Our New Man begins the moment we're born again, but the journey never ends. The time we spend in our earthly tent is a "vapor" as the Bible says, a blink of the eye, a second compared to eternity. And yet, what a second! That is the brief time when the seed of what is to become our imperishable heavenly body is sown, established, and begins growing in our perishable body. Our scant time here on earth is when we have the extraordinary privilege of influencing lives for Christ. It is our time to sow New Man seeds that will take root and form in others as they have in us.

Did Ted and Katie sow the seeds that formed in Tom and Brandy, causing them to bloom and flourish in their new life in Christ? Had Ted and Katie chosen to disown their friendship with Tom and Brandy after being rebuffed for their faith, would Tom's passing have been as victorious? We'll never know for sure on this side of heaven. However, I'm willing to wager that Tom and Brandy's lives would have had an entirely different outcome without Ted and Katie's forgiveness, prayers, love, and friendship. If our eyes could be opened to see all the seeds sown and lives changed by Jesus's followers, we'd be amazed. Someday we'll know and be thrilled to see our human part in the sowing and birthing miracle of the born-again:

"What no eye has seen,
    what no ear has heard,
and what no human mind has conceived"—
    the things God has prepared for those who
        love him....

For now we see only a reflection as in a mirror; then
we shall see face to face. Now I know in part; then I
shall know fully, even as I am fully known. (1 Cor.
2:9; 13:12)

What do you suppose Tom saw and tried to convey to Brandy in
his final moments? Did he see heaven? His mansion there? Was it the
suit of New Man clothes the Spirit had tailored for his homecoming?
Was it something else, something so much more?

Brandy was sure she heard music from the next world but couldn't
experience the glory into which Tom was transitioning. None of us
can because of the gulf that exists between this world and God's
kingdom. Yet we know this much: it will far exceed anything we can
possibly imagine. The book of Revelation gives us some insight:

Then I saw "a new heaven and a new earth," for the
first heaven and the first earth had passed away, and
there was no longer any sea. I saw the Holy City,
the new Jerusalem, coming down out of heaven
from God, prepared as a bride beautifully dressed
for her husband. And I heard a loud voice from the
throne saying, "Look! God's dwelling place is now
among the people, and he will dwell with them.
They will be his people, and God himself will be
with them and be their God. 'He will wipe every
tear from their eyes. There will be no more death'
or mourning or crying or pain, for the old order of
things has passed away."

He who was seated on the throne said, "I am making everything new!"…

Then the angel showed me the river of the water of life, as clear as crystal, flowing from the throne of God and of the Lamb down the middle of the great street of the city. On each side of the river stood the tree of life, bearing twelve crops of fruit, yielding its fruit every month. And the leaves of the tree are for the healing of the nations. No longer will there be any curse. The throne of God and of the Lamb will be in the city, and his servants will serve him. They will see his face, and his name will be on their foreheads. There will be no more night. They will not need the light of a lamp or the light of the sun, for the Lord God will give them light. And they will reign for ever and ever. (Rev. 21:1–5; 22:1–5)

But even Revelation's author, John, couldn't come close to describing heaven in the way Tom was seeing it and in the way we will actually behold the life of our New Man when we arrive there. Why should we even try to grasp heaven? Because it's where we're headed if we're born again. Because our stay there will be infinite. That's worth our attention.

There's a saying that someone can be too heavenly minded to be any earthly good. Well, that may be true in the Old Man paradigm, but not so with our New Man. He is heavenly minded precisely in order to be of earthly good.

Remember Jesus's discussion with Nicodemus? The Lord said, "Very truly I tell you, no one can see the kingdom of God unless they are born again" (John 3:3). Jesus is all about heaven. He was with His Father in heaven in the beginning; He rules over all of heaven; He came from heaven to deliver us from the sin that separated us from God; He went back to heaven after His salvation mission was accomplished; He has prepared a permanent home for us in heaven since our second birth, and He will one day return from heaven to complete His work on earth.

It's only because we're earthbound that heaven is difficult to grasp and we give it so little mindshare. It is a very foreign country to us now. It's like what the Promised Land of Canaan, "flowing with milk and honey" (Ex. 3:8), was to the Israelites while they wandered in the Sinai desert for forty years after Moses led them out of Egypt. Our New Man is familiar with that heavenly real estate and functions as our heaven scout like Joshua and Caleb did in the wilderness days. They scoped out Canaan and reported back to the Israelites how glorious was the Promised Land.

Our New Man occupies both regions, earth and heaven, and is our ever-present reminder of where we're going and what we're about.

Our Old Man has no interest or part in heaven. He couldn't care less and certainly won't be talking it up with his friends. He'll eventually be that old dead skin we discussed, left behind on the side of the road. Our New Man, in contrast, is drawn to heaven and wants as many as possible to join him there. So he sows imperishable New Man seeds into the lives of those around him. Why? It's our New Man job as long as we're in our earthly tent.

I declare to you, brothers and sisters, that flesh
and blood cannot inherit the kingdom of God,
nor does the perishable inherit the imperishable.... For the perishable must clothe itself with
the imperishable, and the mortal with immortal-
ity. When the perishable has been clothed with
the imperishable, and the mortal with immortal-
ity, then the saying that is written will come true:
"Death has been swallowed up in victory." (1 Cor.
15:50, 53–54)

## FIXING OUR EYES

Well, we've come to the end of this phase of our journey. It's strange
that we've traveled a way together without having met in person.
You and I are different, yet very much alike. Different in that our
backgrounds, heritages, professions, interests, experiences, problems,
hopes, dreams, and unique lenses through which we see the world
are all over the map. Alike because we're searching for something
more. More in our marriages and family relationships, friendships,
careers, knowledge, passions, even our daily routines. We could build
long lists of what we want to be more knowledgeable about, better
at, more secure with, or more fulfilled by. We could compare lists
and find many commonalities. Our needs are universal, with few
degrees of separation.

Without knowing each other, we know each other. We recognize one another in smiles, brief glances, small gestures, simple

observations. We recognize each other because we're created by, named, and loved by the same Creator-Father.

The older I get, the more I see this phenomenon at work in my life. I see my marriage in others' marriages. My children and grandchildren in others' children. While I'm a healthy sixty-five-year-old and feeling as strong as ever, I realize that won't last. I see my old age in those at the obvious ends of their lives. I see my wife, still very beautiful, in much older women. I see in them her changing beauty. I imagine us in our eighties and nineties, walking slowly, hand in hand, into one of our favorite restaurants, or down crooked little streets of beloved travel destinations, or up to the front door of a family member's home.

I also see one of us left here after the other has gone on to be with the Lord. That's the hardest and sweetest image of all. Hard because we've come to know the fullness of marriage described in our couples' stories on this journey. Sweet because I know our love will never end and that we'll soon be reunited in heaven.

Heaven. Our New Man country. Forever home to those who have followed and will follow Jesus.

Home to my friend Stan, who recently picked up his New Man suit. Stan had been a close Men's Golf Fellowship partner since our beginning ten years ago. We had much in common. About the same age. Both married to exceptional women who became our best friends. Both of us came to Christ about the same time over forty years ago. Both loving golf and golf friends. Both taking great joy in watching our children's families grow. Both finding profound endgame meaning in exploring New Man possibilities with like-minded friends. We were resources for each other and were comforted knowing the other was out there.

Stan's lymphoma diagnosis came as a shock. He was the picture of health and looked much younger than his sixty-three years. His initial treatments went well. We all expected a full recovery. Over the past several months, however, he developed health issues related to his treatments. Ultimately his heart gave out.

His leaving at this time seems counterintuitive. There was too much for him to do here. He was too important to all of us who counted on his love, friendship, and support. God's timing on this one feels like a mistake. Why didn't He take someone older, less vital, not making as much of an impact here for His kingdom?

But we know God doesn't make mistakes.

In many ways, Stan defined what this book has sought to describe and the destination we are attempting to reach on this journey. There was just something different about him. You sensed the Lord through him in his gentle and vibrant nature. He was a joy to be with. Loved to laugh and have fun, but never at your expense. Always quick to share the hope of Christ within him, but not in ways that made you feel pressured, inferior, or preached to. Just a natural outflowing of an inward reality. Stan was one of those guys with whom you could confide your deepest confidences. You could trust Stan.

A Men's Golf Fellowship discussion group member said it best: "If someone asked me to describe a Christian, Stan would be my answer." I agree with that assessment. Stan was and is my closest personal New Man role model. I'm proud to have had him as my friend and New Man colaborer for our brief ten years together.

Stan had been reading this book and providing comments on chapters. He was honest, deep, and serious about his faith, and I knew he'd call me out on anything that didn't sound genuine or helpful. He was, in a sense, my New Man tuning fork.

I was awaiting Stan's final comments when he died. *That makes sense*, I thought. *Stan's utimate victory speaks for itself.* Then I received an email from Dan, a close mutual friend. Dan said Stan had mentioned to him that he didn't feel the ending had enough of a "punch." Well, Stan, I know from your humility that you wouldn't want to be the "punch" in the ending, but here you are. I know you're now rejoicing in your release and homecoming—separated from your earthly tent to dwell eternally with your faithful Master. I'm certain He welcomed you with those special words you longed to hear: "Well done, thou good and faithful servant."

We look forward to that great moment when we, like Stan, will see our Father face-to-face. In the meantime, as we await our transition from physical life to spiritual life, from the perishable to the imperishable, we're filled with the knowledge of His presence through His Sprit living inside of us.

We desire to know Him better while still in our earthly body, to attract others to Him with transparent New Man natures, to nurture and develop those placed into our care as we mature in faith and knowledge.

We like our New Man job. It's the most exciting, creative work of all. God has chosen to continue His work here by using us, His frail "jars of clay," to sow the seeds, to water the shoots, and to be there when the harvest of imperishable life comes. It's His method.

Jesus Christ's visitation, ministry, sacrificial death, resurrection, exaltation, and reign in His kingdom may go unnoticed by some. However, the momentous event of His life and calling on our lives hasn't escaped you and me on this journey. For a brief time together, He's been the focus of our attention. The object of this journey. The Alpha and Omega, the beginning and the end of our search.

The road is clear. The sun shines. The New Man beckons: "Come see what I see. Let's go discover. Let's follow Him."

> Therefore we do not lose heart. Though outwardly we are wasting away, yet inwardly we are being renewed day by day. For our light and momentary troubles are achieving for us an eternal glory that far outweighs them all. So we fix our eyes not on what is seen, but on what is unseen, since what is seen is temporary, but what is unseen is eternal. (2 Cor. 4:16–18)

# WHAT NOW?

I've sought to make this book an honest, challenging, and fresh look at your New Man. I've attempted to address the questions you need to consider for making the rest of your life the best of your life.

If I was successful, you're asking:

> 1. Who really is in control of my life—the Old Man or the New Man?
> 2. Do I yearn for and seek reconciliation in all my relationships?
> 3. Am I willing to commit to the full New Man job?

So here we are. What now? Let me take a risk here. I believe God is asking more of you. He's not satisfied being in the backseat or, worse, in the trunk of your life. He wants to be up front. The fact is, He wants the wheel—the wheel of your marriage, family relationships, and all your friendships, even the casual ones. He wants to be the focus of your attention and object of your passion, not just your celestial bellhop or triage doctor or subject of your rituals. He wants this not because He needs you, but because you need Him. He wants the highest and best for you.

If this resonates, there's no better time than now—while this journey is fresh on your mind and in your heart—to commit or recommit yourself to living the fullness and substance of your New Man in Christ. You want this. God wants you. Let's ask together.

*God, I'm tired of the power that my lower nature, my Old Man, has had and still has over me. I've lived too long for myself without You—or with You, but only for my convenience. Forgive me for that. I want to shed this Old Man skin and put on my New Man suit that reflects Your nature and witnesses to Your truth. I want the full New Man job—and the transformation necessary to do it well. Help me, by Your Holy Spirit, to live with and for You—fixed on Your kingdom and doing Your work so that I am prepared for that great homecoming! In Jesus's name. Amen.*

*If you would like to engage with me and others on your New Man Journey, visit my blog at www.newmanjourney.com.*